Understanding Rastafari in Correctional Settings
A Guide to Faith, Practice, and Respect

Bryan Rouse   Davidacus Holmes

Copyright © 2025 Sanctuary of the Rastafarian Order All rights reserved

No part of this book may be reproduced, or stored in a retrieval system, or transmitted in any form or by any means, electronic, mechanical, photocopying, recording, or otherwise, without express written permission of the publisher.

ISBN- 979-8-89965-109-0

*Cover design by: Davidacus Holmes
Printed in Canada*

Dedication

This work is humbly dedicated:

To the Elders who have carried the fire of the faith through Babylon's trials,
To the Incarcerated Brethren and Sistren who maintain their livity in the darkest corners of society,
To the Chaplains and Advocates who stand in solidarity with the I-dren and defend the right to practice Rastafari freely,
and
To the Most High Jah Rastafari, whose light guides all trodding, even behind the iron bars.

May this guide serve as a bridge to overstanding, a tool for liberation, and a spark that lights the path forward.

Haile Selassie I — Ever Living, Ever Faithful, Ever Sure.

Preface

Rastafari is often misunderstood. Too often reduced to symbols, stereotypes, or simplified notions of dreadlocks and ganja, the fullness of the faith is rarely acknowledged, especially within institutional systems like correctional facilities. This book was born out of necessity—a call to bring clarity, respect, and truth to the lived experience of Rastafari within these confined spaces.

For many incarcerated brethren and sistren, Rastafari is not a trend or a phase; it is a **way of life**, a covenant with the Most High, and a continuous act of resistance against Babylon's system of oppression. Yet, too frequently, their spiritual needs are dismissed, their practices denied, and their faith mischaracterized.

This guide seeks to build a bridge—between chaplaincy staff and Rastafari practitioners, between policy and lived reality, between misunderstanding and overstanding. It is a tool for those working in correctional settings to approach the faith not as a challenge to be managed, but as a sacred tradition to be honored.

📑 Table of Contents:

1. Introduction to Rastafari: Origins, Beliefs, and Global Influence
2. Rastafari in Correctional Institutions: Challenges and Misconceptions
3. The Nazirite Vow – Foundation of the Faith
4. Ital – The Sacred Diet of Rastafari
5. Worship, Prayer, and Spiritual Practices
6. The Role and Symbolism of Head Coverings
7. Dreadlocks: A Spiritual Commitment, Not a Fashion Statement
8. Rastafari Language and Communication Styles
9. The Importance of Nature, Herbal Use, and Holistic Healing
10. Rastafari and the Bible: Scriptural Foundations of the Faith
11. Music and Chanting in Rastafari Worship
12. Holy Days and Observances in the Rastafari Calendar
13. Discrimination and Legal Rights: Rastafari and Religious Protections
14. Best Practices for Correctional Staff: Cultural Competency and Respect
15. Building Bridges: Supporting Spiritual Rehabilitation for Rastafari Inmates

📖 Introduction

The Rastafari movement, often misunderstood or misrepresented in mainstream narratives, is a deeply spiritual and culturally rooted faith that emphasizes a life of holiness, natural living, and liberation. Emerging in the 1930s in Jamaica, Rastafari was born from a desire to reclaim African identity and spiritual sovereignty in the wake of colonialism and systemic oppression. For many adherents, Rastafari is not just a religion — it is a **way of life**, encompassing diet, dress, hair, language, and worldview.

In correctional settings, individuals who identify with the Rastafari faith often encounter a range of challenges: from the denial of access to sacred dietary needs to restrictions on hair, head coverings, or religious gatherings. These restrictions are not merely inconveniences — they strike at the heart of the Rastafari identity and spiritual practice. This guide seeks to bridge the gap between institutional policies and religious accommodations by providing a respectful, educational, and actionable resource for correctional administrators, officers, and staff.

Understanding Rastafari within the correctional environment requires more than just policy adjustments — it requires **compassion, education, and a willingness to acknowledge the depth of this faith**. Rastafari practitioners often take a Nazirite vow — a sacred commitment that includes the growing of dreadlocks, abstention from alcohol, meat, and certain behaviors, and a life dedicated to spiritual purity. Their diet, known as **Ital**, is rooted in natural, plant-based foods free from additives, chemicals, or preservatives. Worship can include communal gatherings, drumming, chanting, and reading from the Bible, particularly the Old Testament, which holds deep spiritual significance.

This guide will unpack the key elements of Rastafari — not only its theological beliefs but also the cultural expressions that are inseparable from the faith. It will clarify the importance of dreadlocks, head coverings, and the rejection of synthetic or processed substances. It will also examine how prison policies can unintentionally violate the religious rights of Rastafari inmates and provide actionable strategies to support their freedom of religious expression.

At its core, Rastafari is a faith of **peace, reverence for life, and resistance against oppression**. Incarcerated Rastafari adherents often maintain a strong commitment to their beliefs, which can be a source of strength, rehabilitation, and spiritual development. By better understanding the principles of this faith, correctional systems can contribute to an environment that fosters respect, dignity, and holistic rehabilitation.

This book is both a **manual and a bridge** — offering corrections professionals the knowledge they need to treat Rastafari adherents with respect while supporting inmates in maintaining a vital connection to their spiritual path. Respect for religious freedom is not only a legal obligation — it is a **moral one** that reflects the highest values of justice, equity, and human dignity.

Great! Let's dive into **Chapter 1**, laying the foundation by exploring the **origins**, **beliefs**, and **global influence** of the Rastafari faith. This chapter sets the tone for the entire guide and provides crucial context for understanding the movement within correctional institutions.

📖 Chapter 1: Introduction to Rastafari: Origins, Beliefs, and Global Influence

Origins of the Rastafari Movement

The Rastafari movement began in **Jamaica in the 1930s**, a response to the social, political, and spiritual dislocation caused by colonialism, slavery, and the post-emancipation struggles of African descendants in the Caribbean. Rastafari emerged from a mixture of **Afrocentric ideologies**, **Christian theology**, and **Pan-African philosophy**, rooted in the desire to reclaim African identity and divinity after centuries of oppression.

One of the most influential figures in the formation of Rastafari ideology was **Marcus Mosiah Garvey**, a Jamaican political leader, publisher, and Pan-Africanist who championed Black pride, self-reliance, and repatriation to Africa. Though not a Rasta himself, Garvey is often considered a **prophet within the faith**. His teachings, particularly the prophecy that Black people should "look to Africa where a Black king shall be crowned," were interpreted by early Rastafari adherents as the foretelling of the **coronation of Emperor Haile Selassie I** of Ethiopia in 1930.

Selassie, born Ras Tafari Makonnen, became the centerpiece of the movement. To Rastafari, he is not just a king or emperor — he is **divine**, the living God, referred to as **Jah Rastafari**. His reign symbolized the realization of prophecy and the promise of redemption for African people worldwide. Despite Selassie's own Ethiopian Orthodox Christian beliefs and his disavowal of divinity, Rastafari adherents continue to revere him as the returned Messiah of the Bible.

Core Beliefs of Rastafari

Though the movement has no centralized church or singular doctrine, several key beliefs unify its followers across the world:

1. Haile Selassie I is the Living God (Jah)

Rastafari reveres Haile Selassie as the earthly incarnation of God, or **Jah**, and the fulfillment of biblical prophecy. He is seen as the rightful ruler and redeemer of the African diaspora.

2. Zion and Babylon

Rastas view **Zion** (often symbolized by Ethiopia or Africa more broadly) as a spiritual homeland, a place of peace, righteousness, and divine presence. In contrast, **Babylon** refers to the oppressive systems of the West — colonialism, materialism, racism, and spiritual corruption. Rastafari emphasizes a rejection of Babylon and a return, spiritually or physically, to Zion.

3. The Divinity of the Black Race

Rastafari affirms the **divine identity and dignity of African people**, countering centuries of dehumanization. The movement emphasizes the reclamation of African history, pride, and identity, often interpreting the Bible through an Afrocentric lens.

4. Natural Living

The principle of **living naturally** is central to Rastafari practice. This includes wearing natural hairstyles like dreadlocks, eating an **Ital** (natural, plant-based) diet, and avoiding artificial substances, including alcohol, drugs, and processed foods.

5. Livity (Righteous Living)

"Livity" refers to a way of life in harmony with the divine, nature, and fellow human beings. It encompasses ethical behavior, respect for all life, and spiritual discipline.

Global Expansion and Cultural Influence

While Rastafari began in Jamaica, its influence has since spread worldwide, especially through **music, cultural expression, and activism**. The international success of artists like **Bob Marley**, **Peter Tosh**, and **Burning Spear** brought Rastafari philosophy into global consciousness. Marley, in particular, became a spiritual ambassador for the faith, using reggae as a vehicle to share messages of liberation, unity, and divine truth.

Today, Rastafari communities can be found in **Africa, North America, Europe, South America, and the Caribbean**. While the core principles remain consistent, local expressions may vary. Some adherents focus more heavily on the repatriation message, while others emphasize ethical living or scriptural study. Despite differences, the spiritual lineage remains rooted in the African experience, biblical prophecy, and resistance to oppression.

Rastafari as a Way of Life

Rastafari is not merely a religion in the conventional sense — it is a **way of life**. Unlike institutionalized religions with churches, clergy, or formal hierarchies, Rastafari places emphasis on personal connection to the divine, communal reasoning, and individual discipline. The movement is **non-dogmatic**, which means that personal revelation and interpretation are central to spiritual growth.

This way of life encompasses everything from **how one eats (Ital)**, to **how one dresses**, to the **language one uses** (often replacing words associated with oppression with terms reflecting divinity and empowerment — e.g., "I and I" instead of "you and me").

Common Misconceptions

Due to media portrayal, law enforcement biases, and lack of education, Rastafari is often misunderstood. Common misconceptions include:

- **"It's just a cultural or musical movement."**
  In truth, Rastafari is a deeply spiritual practice rooted in theology, scripture, and divine revelation.
- **"All Rastas smoke ganja recreationally."**
  While some Rastas use **ganja (herb)** sacramentally for meditation and prayer, it is not a recreational drug. Its use is deeply spiritual and regulated by strict principles.
- **"Dreadlocks are just a fashion statement."**
  Dreadlocks are a **sacred expression** of the Nazirite vow, representing a covenant with Jah. Cutting them is akin to a religious violation.
- **"Rastas reject the Bible."**
  On the contrary, Rastas revere the Bible, particularly the **Old Testament**, though they often interpret it from an Afrocentric and prophetic lens.

Rastafari in the Correctional System

As Rastafari continues to grow globally, it also finds adherents within correctional institutions. Incarcerated Rastas often face challenges in maintaining their spiritual practices due to lack of awareness or accommodation by prison staff. Practices such as wearing head coverings, maintaining dreadlocks, eating an Ital diet, and observing sacred rituals are integral to their spiritual health and identity.

Understanding Rastafari is essential not only for **upholding religious rights** but also for fostering an environment of **respect, rehabilitation, and personal growth**. In many cases, adherence to Rastafari principles has helped incarcerated individuals find purpose, discipline, and spiritual resilience.

Conclusion

Rastafari is a living, breathing faith rooted in the quest for truth, dignity, and spiritual liberation. Far more than a cultural phenomenon, it is a powerful spiritual system that has inspired millions across the world to seek deeper meaning in their lives. For correctional staff and administrators, understanding this movement is critical to ensuring that the **religious rights of Rastafari inmates are protected** and that their spiritual needs are met with dignity and respect.

This chapter serves as the groundwork for exploring deeper aspects of the faith — from the sacred **Nazirite vow** and **Ital diet**, to the significance of **head coverings, dreadlocks**, and **spiritual worship**.

✅ **Next Chapter: Chapter 2 – Rastafari in Correctional Institutions: Challenges and Misconceptions**

Would you like me to continue with Chapter 2 now?

Perfect! Let's move forward with **Chapter 2**, focusing on the specific realities of **Rastafari adherents in correctional institutions**. This chapter addresses the challenges they face, the common misconceptions held by staff or other inmates, and why **understanding and respecting their faith** is essential to upholding human rights and fostering true rehabilitation.

📖 Chapter 2: Rastafari in Correctional Institutions: Challenges and Misconceptions

Introduction

Correctional facilities are designed to enforce discipline, protect the public, and offer rehabilitative services. However, in doing so, these institutions often impose uniform structures that can conflict with individual religious and cultural practices. For **Rastafari adherents**, incarceration presents unique spiritual challenges. The Rastafari way of life — deeply intertwined with identity, diet, hair, language, and worship — often clashes with the routines and policies of prison environments.

This chapter explores the **practical and spiritual difficulties** that Rastafari individuals face while incarcerated, the **misunderstandings that contribute to discrimination**, and the **legal and ethical obligations** that correctional institutions have to accommodate religious practices.

Institutional Challenges for Rastafari Inmates

1. The Sacredness of Dreadlocks

Rastafari men and women who take the **Nazirite vow** allow their hair to grow freely into dreadlocks, which symbolize their covenant with **Jah** (God). In many prison systems, however, hair length is regulated under grooming policies meant to enforce cleanliness or uniformity.

Being forced to cut dreadlocks is not a simple matter of hygiene — it is a **deep spiritual violation**. It can be compared to demanding that someone renounce their religious identity or destroy a sacred artifact. In many instances, Rastafari inmates have endured **disciplinary actions**, **segregation**, or **forced haircuts**, despite constitutional protections for religious freedom.

"When they cut my locks, it was like they cut a part of my soul." — Incarcerated Rastafari Practitioner

2. Head Coverings and Religious Identity

Head coverings, such as **crowns, turbans, or tams**, are worn by Rastafari adherents as **symbols of spiritual authority**, **modesty**, and **connection to the divine**. In correctional settings, these are often prohibited due to security concerns, mistaken for gang affiliations, or misunderstood as unnecessary personal items.

Denying head coverings not only undermines the Rasta's dignity but also strips them of an important religious symbol, often leading to disciplinary consequences for refusing to remove them.

3. Dietary Restrictions and Ital Living

Rastafari dietary practice, known as **Ital**, emphasizes **natural, unprocessed, plant-based foods**, free from chemicals, artificial ingredients, salt, or meat. In prison, where meals are highly processed, heavy in preservatives, and often meat-based, Rastas frequently struggle to maintain their dietary vows.

Requests for **special religious diets** are sometimes denied or inconsistently honored, leading to spiritual distress and nutritional challenges. In some institutions, Rasta inmates are labeled as "picky" or "troublesome" for refusing meals, when in fact, they are exercising a **core tenet of their faith**.

4. Access to Religious Materials and Worship

Unlike many other faiths, Rastafari worship does not revolve around chapels or formal sermons. Instead, it includes **reasoning sessions**, **chanting**, **drumming**, **reading of Psalms**, and meditative use of **herbs** (such as cannabis, though its use in prison is restricted).

In many institutions, Rasta inmates are denied **space for communal worship**, **access to spiritual books**, or the **right to gather** for religious purposes. Their practices are sometimes dismissed as "unofficial" or "not real religion," despite falling under protected constitutional freedoms in many jurisdictions.

Common Misconceptions and Harmful Stereotypes

Misconception 1: "Rasta is not a real religion."

Because Rastafari lacks formal clergy or centralized churches, it is sometimes dismissed as a philosophy or lifestyle rather than a legitimate religious system. In reality, Rastafari is **deeply spiritual**, centered on the worship of **Jah**, scriptural interpretation, and spiritual discipline.

Misconception 2: "All Rastas just want to smoke marijuana."

While the sacramental use of **herb** is part of some Rasta practices, it is not a requirement, and it is never used recreationally in authentic Rastafari worship. Incarcerated Rastas understand the limitations placed on herb use in correctional settings but still face **stigma and suspicion** around drug use.

Misconception 3: "Rastas are rebellious or noncompliant."

Many Rastafari inmates are labeled as uncooperative when they stand firm in their religious beliefs, such as refusing to cut their locks or eat non-Ital food. In truth, they are demonstrating **deep faith, not defiance**. Institutional misunderstanding of religious conviction often leads to **punishment instead of accommodation**.

Misconception 4: "Dreadlocks and head coverings are gang identifiers."

This is a damaging stereotype. While some gangs have adopted certain symbols or aesthetics, **Rastafari dreadlocks and turbans are sacred**, not criminal. Equating spiritual symbols with gang affiliation contributes to racial and religious profiling.

Legal Protections and Religious Rights

"Legal Protections and Religious Rights" section with a focus on the **Canadian legal framework**, including references to the **Canadian Charter of Rights and Freedoms, Corrections and Conditional Release Act (CCRA)**, and relevant policies that apply within **Correctional Service Canada (CSC)**.

Canada is a country that upholds **freedom of religion** as a constitutional right, including for individuals in correctional settings. Incarcerated persons do not lose their right to practice their faith while serving time. For **Rastafari adherents**, this means the right to wear religious head coverings, maintain dreadlocks as a spiritual vow, follow an Ital diet, and participate in spiritual practices must be respected, provided they do not pose undue safety or security risks.

📜 1. The Canadian Charter of Rights and Freedoms

The **Canadian Charter of Rights and Freedoms**, entrenched in the **Constitution Act, 1982**, guarantees the **freedom of conscience and religion** under **Section 2(a)**. This right applies to **all individuals**, including those who are incarcerated.

This means that Rastafari inmates have the constitutional right to:

- Hold and express their religious beliefs;
- Engage in spiritual practices such as wearing head coverings or dreadlocks;
- Request religious diets in line with Ital principles;
- Access spiritual materials and participate in religious gatherings.

Any **limitation of these rights** by correctional institutions must be **justifiable under Section 1 of the Charter**, which allows reasonable limits only if they can be demonstrably justified in a free and democratic society. In other words, **prison authorities must prove that restricting a religious practice is necessary, minimal, and proportionate.**

🏛 2. Corrections and Conditional Release Act (CCRA)

Under the **Corrections and Conditional Release Act (CCRA)** — the primary legislation governing federal corrections in Canada — there are clear provisions protecting inmates' spiritual rights.

Section 75 of the CCRA specifically states:

"An inmate has the right to reasonable opportunities to freely and openly practice their religion or spirituality."

Additionally, **Section 83** outlines the need to respect and support **cultural and spiritual diversity** within the correctional system, including Indigenous and other minority faith traditions such as Rastafari.

This legal framework places an obligation on **Correctional Service Canada (CSC)** to make reasonable accommodations for religious practice, including:

- Access to spiritual advisors or elders;
- Time and space for religious observances;
- Religious or spiritual items (head coverings, prayer cloths, sacred books);
- Dietary requirements based on faith.

◼ 3. CSC Policy and Religious Accommodation

Correctional Service Canada has a formal **Commissioner's Directive 726: Correctional Programs** and **Commissioner's Directive 767: Religious and Spiritual Accommodation**, which outline responsibilities and protocols for supporting religious freedom.

Under these policies:

- Inmates are entitled to **spiritual counselling and group worship** with recognized spiritual leaders or chaplains;
- Requests for **religious diets** (e.g., Ital, vegetarian, or vegan) must be processed and reasonably accommodated;
- **Grooming exemptions** may be granted on religious grounds, including for the maintenance of dreadlocks or facial hair;
- **Religious head coverings** must be permitted unless they pose a demonstrated security risk, in which

case accommodations should be made wherever possible.

CSC recognizes that religion and spirituality are **key components of rehabilitation**, especially for individuals from **marginalized or racialized communities**, such as those who practice Rastafari.

⚖️ 4. Legal Precedents and Human Rights Protections

In addition to the Charter and CCRA, **human rights legislation**—such as the **Canadian Human Rights Act**—protects individuals against **discrimination on the basis of religion or creed**.

If a Rastafari inmate is denied the right to wear a head covering, maintain dreadlocks, or follow an Ital diet **without reasonable justification**, this could be grounds for a **human rights complaint** or **judicial review**.

Legal precedents in Canadian law have repeatedly upheld that **correctional facilities must accommodate religious beliefs** unless they can demonstrate that doing so would cause undue hardship, such as a serious threat to safety or security.

🌸 The Duty to Accommodate

The concept of the **duty to accommodate** is central to religious freedom in Canada. This means that institutions, including prisons, must take all reasonable steps to **adjust rules, policies, or procedures** to allow individuals to practice their religion.

In the context of Rastafari:

- If the standard grooming policy requires haircuts, exceptions must be made for those who keep dreadlocks as part of their **Nazirite vow**.
- If the meal plan includes meat or processed food, alternatives must be made available for those following the **Ital diet**.
- If headgear is banned, allowances must be created for **religious head coverings** like crowns, tams, or wraps.

Accommodations should only be denied if there is **clear, documented evidence** that the request would cause serious disruption, risk, or unreasonable burden.

Institutional Best Practice

To comply with Canadian law and uphold ethical standards, correctional institutions should:

- Maintain up-to-date **training programs** for staff on religious diversity, including lesser-known faiths like Rastafari;
- Ensure **chaplaincy services** are inclusive and responsive to the needs of Rastafari practitioners;
- Establish protocols for responding promptly and respectfully to **requests for religious accommodation**;
- Include **Rastafari resources** (texts, literature, music) in institutional libraries and chaplain offices;
- Foster a **non-discriminatory environment**, where inmates are not mocked, punished, or isolated for expressing their faith.

Conclusion

In Canada, the right to practice one's religion is **constitutionally protected**, even behind bars. Rastafari inmates must be afforded **respect and accommodations** that allow them to live in alignment with their spiritual beliefs. Correctional staff, administrators, and policy makers have a legal and moral responsibility to ensure that **faith is not compromised by confinement**.

By understanding and upholding the religious rights of Rastafari adherents, the correctional system moves closer to its goals of **equity, rehabilitation, and human dignity** — values that lie at the heart of Canada's justice system.

However, despite these laws, many Rasta inmates continue to face **denial of rights**, often due to ignorance rather than intentional discrimination. Correctional facilities must take proactive steps to **train staff, update policies**, and **respect religious diversity**.

The Role of Correctional Staff and Administrators

Creating a respectful environment for Rastafari inmates begins with **education and awareness**. Correctional officers and administrators should be trained to recognize the key tenets of Rastafari and understand how those beliefs manifest in daily life.

Key Responsibilities:

- **Respect grooming exemptions** for religious hair practices.
- **Permit head coverings** when they are religious in nature.
- **Provide access to Ital meals** or vegan/vegetarian options that align with Ital principles.
- **Allow group worship**, access to sacred texts, and meaningful religious expression.

- **Avoid discriminatory labeling**, stereotyping, or punitive responses to spiritual practices.

By acknowledging the **dignity of faith**, correctional institutions can become spaces of transformation and growth rather than suppression.

Inmate Testimonies: The Human Side

"Rastafari saved my life in here. It gave me purpose, discipline, and a reason to rise above the system. But every day is a fight just to be myself."

"I've been written up for refusing to take off my headwrap. They call it noncompliance. I call it righteousness."

These voices from behind the walls reveal the emotional and spiritual cost of being denied the ability to live one's faith fully. Rastafari, for many inmates, is a **source of hope, order, and transformation** — an internal liberation that exists even behind bars.

Conclusion

Incarceration is, by design, a place of restriction — but religious expression must not be among the freedoms lost. For Rastafari adherents, faith is a lifeline, a compass, and a sacred duty. When correctional systems fail to recognize the legitimacy and depth of this spiritual path, they not only violate legal rights but also contribute to spiritual harm and institutional distrust.

This chapter has revealed that **most issues facing Rastafari inmates stem from misunderstanding**, not malice. The solution lies in **education, dialogue, and**

respect — creating correctional environments that uphold religious freedom while maintaining safety and order.

As we move into the next chapters, we will explore in detail the **spiritual foundations** of the Rastafari faith, beginning with the **Nazirite vow**, which underpins the commitment to dreadlocks, abstinence, and spiritual purity.

---

*Chapter 3, exploring the **Nazirite Vow** — one of the most sacred and defining elements of the **Rastafari faith**. This chapter unpacks the biblical roots of the vow, how it is lived out in Rastafari culture, and why it's especially critical to respect this practice in **correctional settings**.*

📖 Chapter 3: The Nazirite Vow – Foundation of the Faith

Introduction

The **Nazirite Vow** is not merely a symbolic practice in the Rastafari tradition — it is the **spiritual foundation** upon which much of the faith is built. Originating from the **Bible**, this vow forms a covenant between the individual and **Jah (God)**, marking a deep commitment to purity, spiritual discipline, and separation from worldly corruption. For Rastafari adherents, especially those incarcerated, the Nazirite vow becomes a powerful act of **inner liberation**, often maintained with unshakable conviction in the face of institutional pressure.

In this chapter, we will explore the biblical roots of the Nazirite vow, how it shapes Rastafari identity, its practical manifestations, and the vital importance of **religious accommodation** in correctional facilities.

Biblical Origins of the Nazirite Vow

The concept of the **Nazirite vow** (sometimes spelled Nazarite) comes from the **Old Testament**, specifically **Numbers 6:1–21**. In this passage, individuals are invited to set themselves apart for a period of dedication to God. While originally a temporary vow, many Rastafari take it as a **lifelong commitment.**

"When either a man or woman shall separate themselves to vow a vow of a Nazarite, to separate themselves unto the LORD..."
— Numbers 6:2 (KJV)

The vow includes three major commandments:

1. **Abstaining from all products of the grapevine** — including wine, vinegar, grapes, and raisins.
2. **Refraining from cutting the hair of the head** during the period of the vow.
3. **Avoiding contact with dead bodies**, even those of family members, to maintain spiritual cleanliness.

In Rastafari, these principles are interpreted not only literally, but also symbolically — representing a broader commitment to **spiritual discipline, purity, and separation from "Babylon"**, the corrupt system of the world.

The Nazirite Vow in Rastafari

Rastafari adopts the Nazirite vow as a **central spiritual discipline**. It is not enforced, but chosen — a sign of personal dedication to **Jah Rastafari**, a lifestyle of livity (righteous living), and a form of resistance to oppressive systems.

1. Dreadlocks: A Sacred Covenant

The most visible sign of the Nazirite vow in Rastafari is the wearing of **dreadlocks**. These are not simply a hairstyle or cultural expression — they are the physical **manifestation of the vow**. The refusal to cut or comb the hair is a direct reflection of the commandment found in **Numbers 6:5**:

"All the days of the vow of his separation there shall no razor come upon his head."

Dreadlocks symbolize:

- A sacred contract between the individual and Jah;
- Strength and natural wisdom (mirroring the biblical figure **Samson**, whose strength was in his hair);
- Rejection of vanity, conformity, and Babylonian values.

In correctional settings, forced haircuts are not just policy violations — they are **spiritual violations**. Cutting a Rasta's locks without consent is akin to demanding they **break their covenant with God**. This act can cause deep psychological trauma, spiritual alienation, and loss of identity.

---

2. Abstinence and Purity

The vow also requires abstention from **alcohol, unclean foods**, and contact with **spiritually impure elements**. Rastafari extend this to modern interpretations of purity, including:

- **No consumption of meat or blood**;
- **Avoidance of synthetic drugs**, unless medically required;

- **Refraining from toxic behavior**, including violence, lying, or exploitation.

For many Rastas, this vow becomes a **code of ethical conduct** — one that promotes inner peace, dignity, and divine connection. In prison, where corruption, violence, and spiritual darkness can be rampant, the Nazirite vow becomes a **shield of righteousness**, a way to rise above the system spiritually, even while being confined physically.

3. Separation from Babylon

In biblical times, those under the Nazirite vow were expected to **separate themselves** from worldly distractions. In Rastafari, this is expressed through conscious rejection of **Babylon** — the oppressive, exploitative systems of the world, including racism, capitalism, colonialism, and the prison-industrial complex.

The vow inspires Rastas to:

- Remain uncorrupted by the prison environment;
- Refuse to participate in unethical behavior;
- Use incarceration as a time of **spiritual reflection and cleansing**.

Living the Vow in Correctional Settings

Incarcerated Rastafari adherents often face tremendous pressure to compromise their faith — from being forced to cut their hair, to being denied access to Ital food, to being mocked or punished for their beliefs. Yet, many remain **steadfast in their vow**, using it as a daily spiritual discipline and source of strength.

Common Institutional Challenges:

- **Mandatory grooming policies** that conflict with the commandment not to cut hair.
- **Labeling of dreadlocks as gang affiliation**, leading to punishment or isolation.
- **Lack of understanding of the vow's spiritual significance**, reducing it to a cultural preference.
- **Mockery or disrespect** from staff or other inmates who do not understand its religious importance.

In some institutions, Rastas have been forced to cut their hair under threat of solitary confinement, denied program participation, or excluded from chapel services. These actions not only violate religious rights but also **erode the rehabilitative goals** of the correctional system.

Spiritual Impact of the Vow

For Rasta inmates, the Nazirite vow can be a **path to healing and transformation**. It instills:

- **Self-discipline** in environments where control is often taken away;
- **Purpose and meaning**, anchoring them in a divine mission;
- **Spiritual resilience**, even in the face of hardship.

Many Rastas report that living the vow in prison keeps them focused, grounded, and spiritually connected — making it not only a religious commitment, but a **source of strength** for personal rehabilitation.

"This vow is my covenant. Without it, I would lose myself in here."
— Rastafari inmate, Ontario

Best Practices for Correctional Institutions

Respecting the Nazirite vow is not only a legal obligation (under the Canadian Charter and CSC policy), but also a matter of **human dignity and religious freedom**. Institutions that wish to support faith-based rehabilitation should:

- **Allow exemptions to grooming policies** for those under the vow.
- **Educate staff** about the spiritual importance of dreadlocks and other vow-related practices.
- **Permit head coverings** that reflect spiritual modesty.
- **Accommodate dietary needs** aligned with the vow's requirements.
- **Avoid disciplinary action** based on misunderstood religious practices.

By doing so, correctional institutions affirm the principle that **rehabilitation includes spiritual development** and that faith-based paths should be nurtured, not obstructed.

Conclusion

The **Nazirite vow** is a sacred, lifelong commitment for many Rastafari believers — a declaration of holiness, separation from corruption, and dedication to righteous living. Incarcerated Rastas who uphold this vow are not engaging in rebellion or noncompliance; they are exercising **spiritual sovereignty** in one of the only ways available to them.

To respect this vow is to recognize the **depth of Rastafari spirituality** and the **power of faith in human transformation**. It is an opportunity for correctional systems to move beyond punitive models and embrace a more **holistic approach to rehabilitation** — one that honors the dignity, faith, and humanity of all.

Chapter 4, *diving into one of the most essential and often misunderstood elements of the Rastafari faith: the **Ital diet**. This chapter will explore its spiritual foundations, practical expressions, health implications, and the challenges of maintaining Ital in correctional environments. It also offers guidance for correctional institutions on how to support Rastafari inmates in adhering to this sacred dietary law.*

📖 Chapter 4: Ital – The Sacred Diet of Rastafari
Introduction

The **Ital diet** is more than a health choice — it is a **spiritual obligation** deeply rooted in Rastafari theology, cultural identity, and the principle of *livity*, or righteous living. For those within the faith, consuming only what is clean, natural, and divinely aligned is a fundamental part of their covenant with **Jah (God)**. Ital eating is a direct reflection of Rastafari beliefs in purity, harmony with nature, and resistance to Babylonian systems of control — including industrialized food production, processed goods, and chemical consumption.

In correctional settings, maintaining an Ital diet can be one of the most difficult aspects of practicing the Rastafari faith. Institutional meals are rarely designed with Ital principles in mind, leading to conflict, spiritual hardship, and even disciplinary action when inmates refuse to eat what is provided.

This chapter explores the **origins, philosophy, and real-world application** of the Ital diet, while providing correctional administrators with the knowledge and tools needed to **accommodate** this vital spiritual practice.

What is Ital?

The word **Ital** is derived from the word "vital" — stripped of the **Babylonian 'v'** to reflect purity in language and thought. Ital means **natural, pure, and alive**. It is not simply vegetarianism or veganism; rather, it is a holistic approach to eating that is **guided by spiritual law**, not just physical health.

Key Principles of Ital:

1. **Natural and Unprocessed**
   Food must be free of chemicals, additives, and artificial substances. Rastas avoid canned goods, processed sugars, preservatives, and anything synthetic.
2. **No Meat or Blood**
   Many Rastas are **strict vegetarians or vegans**, rejecting the consumption of meat or animal products because they are associated with death, violence, and spiritual impurity.
3. **No Salt (in strict forms)**
   Some practitioners avoid **iodized salt**, especially refined salt, as it is seen as an unnatural and addictive substance. Natural sea salt may be used minimally, depending on personal conviction.
4. **No Alcohol or Drugs**
   Ital extends beyond food. Rastas reject alcohol, tobacco, and synthetic drugs (except when medically necessary), as these cloud the mind and spirit.
5. **Locally Grown and Organic**
   Whenever possible, food is sourced from nature — ideally homegrown or locally produced, to maintain a direct connection with the Earth.

Biblical and Spiritual Roots

The Ital diet is influenced by **biblical law**, especially the dietary guidelines found in the **Books of Leviticus and Deuteronomy**, which speak to clean and unclean foods. Rastafari draws heavily from these scriptures, emphasizing the connection between bodily purity and spiritual strength.

"And the Lord said... Ye shall therefore sanctify yourselves, and ye shall be holy; for I am holy."
— Leviticus 11:44

Ital eating is a way to sanctify the body — the **temple of Jah**. Food is not just fuel; it is a **sacred medium** that connects the physical body to the spiritual realm. To consume death (meat, blood, preservatives) is to ingest **Babylonian energy**, which Rastas see as spiritually harmful.

Ital as a Form of Resistance

In addition to spiritual discipline, Ital represents a powerful **form of cultural and political resistance**. The processed, fast-food-heavy, consumer-driven diet promoted by global systems is viewed by Rastas as a tool of **Babylon**, meant to weaken the body and dull the mind.

By eating Ital, Rastas reject:

- The industrial food system;
- Colonial patterns of consumption;
- Western notions of health and nutrition;
- The commodification of nature.

In prison, this resistance becomes even more profound. Eating Ital under state control is a **daily act of faith and self-liberation**. It allows Rastafari inmates to maintain their identity and resist spiritual domination, even while confined physically.

Ital in Practice: What Does a Typical Ital Diet Include?

An Ital diet may vary slightly depending on region and individual interpretation, but common elements include:

- **Fruits and Vegetables**: Fresh, organic, and often raw;
- **Whole Grains**: Brown rice, oats, millet, quinoa;
- **Legumes**: Lentils, peas, chickpeas, and kidney beans;
- **Herbs and Spices**: Natural seasonings like turmeric, ginger, garlic, thyme;
- **Coconut and Plant-Based Oils**: For cooking and nutrition;
- **No Processed Foods**: Including white flour, refined sugar, artificial flavors;
- **No Dairy or Eggs** (for most strict Ital followers).

Some Rastas may permit small allowances for fish or dairy based on personal belief, but the general commitment is toward **natural, plant-based eating**.

Challenges of Maintaining Ital in Correctional Institutions

For Rastafari inmates, adhering to the Ital diet can be extremely difficult behind bars, where the **daily meal options** typically include:

- Processed meats or fish;
- White bread and sugary snacks;
- Canned vegetables and fruit packed in syrup;
- Artificial flavors and preservatives.

Common Challenges:

1. **Lack of Dietary Options**
   Most prison kitchens are not equipped to prepare fresh, whole-food meals without salt, meat, or preservatives.
2. **Mislabeling of Requests**
   Ital requests are often confused with veganism or vegetarianism, missing the **spiritual intent** behind the practice.
3. **Disciplinary Repercussions**
   Inmates who reject meals may be viewed as noncompliant or difficult, leading to infractions or loss of privileges.
4. **Lack of Understanding Among Staff**
   Without cultural training, staff may not grasp the religious significance of Ital, leading to unintentional discrimination.

Legal and Institutional Support for Ital in Canada

As discussed in Chapter 2, the **Canadian Charter of Rights and Freedoms** protects the right to religious practice, including dietary observances. Under the **Corrections and Conditional Release Act** and CSC policy (especially **Commissioner's Directive 767**), institutions are required to **accommodate religious diets**, unless doing so would pose an undue hardship.

A properly supported Ital diet in prison may involve:

- Providing **vegan meals** with fresh vegetables and whole grains;
- Ensuring **no cross-contamination** with meat products;

- Avoiding **processed ingredients**, where feasible;
- Respecting inmate requests for **religiously motivated diets**, not merely health preferences.

By recognizing Ital as a **religious necessity**, correctional institutions uphold both legal and ethical obligations.

Case Example: Ital in Action

A Rastafari inmate in British Columbia submitted a religious accommodation request to receive Ital meals. Initially misunderstood as a vegan diet, the institution offered processed soy products and meat substitutes. The inmate respectfully declined, explaining that Ital requires whole foods and rejects synthetic ingredients. After clarification through a religious advisor and chaplain, the facility adjusted the menu to include simple rice, lentils, fresh vegetables, and fruit, restoring the inmate's access to spiritual nourishment.

This example demonstrates that **clear communication and cultural literacy** can result in successful accommodation without disrupting institutional order.

Best Practices for Correctional Institutions

1. **Recognize Ital as a Religious Diet**
   Not just a health preference — it is an essential part of Rastafari belief and livity.
2. **Provide Simple, Whole-Food Options**
   Rice, legumes, vegetables, and fruit are affordable, nutritious, and align with Ital principles.
3. **Avoid Assumptions**
   Do not equate Ital with Western veganism or assume all Rastas eat the same.

4. **Consult Spiritual Advisors or Chaplains**
   Use culturally informed guidance when questions arise about religious accommodation.
5. **Train Kitchen Staff and Administrators**
   Cultural competence is key to avoiding conflict and ensuring religious respect.

Conclusion

The Ital diet is a sacred manifestation of the Rastafari faith — a daily discipline rooted in scripture, natural law, and spiritual purification. For Rasta inmates, eating Ital is not a preference, but a **sacred obligation** that affirms their identity, dignity, and connection to Jah.

Correctional institutions that understand and accommodate Ital are not just complying with law — they are honoring the humanity and spiritual resilience of those in their care. In doing so, they contribute to a **rehabilitative environment**, where religious identity is protected, and spiritual growth is possible.

***Chapter 5**, where we explore the heart of the Rastafari spiritual experience — **worship, prayer, and daily spiritual practices**. This chapter focuses on how Rastafari practitioners commune with **Jah**, what forms their worship takes, and how these sacred rituals can be recognized and supported in **correctional settings**.*

📖 Chapter 5: Worship, Prayer, and Spiritual Practices in Rastafari

Introduction

Worship in the Rastafari faith is not confined to specific buildings or rigid liturgies. Instead, it is a **living, breathing expression** of the individual's relationship with **Jah (God)**, expressed through **meditation, chanting, drumming, reading scripture**, and **daily righteous living**. Rastafari spirituality is dynamic and personal, grounded in the Bible — especially the Psalms — and infused with African heritage, Ethiopian traditions, and resistance to Babylonian oppression.

In correctional environments, Rastafari worship practices are often **misunderstood**, **dismissed**, or **ignored altogether**. The lack of formal church services or ordained clergy leads some institutions to underestimate the depth of Rasta devotion. However, for Rastafari inmates, these spiritual disciplines are **essential lifelines** that sustain mental clarity, spiritual health, and moral focus.

This chapter offers a deeper understanding of how Rastafari worship works, how it differs from mainstream religious expressions, and how it can be meaningfully and respectfully supported in correctional institutions.

Foundations of Worship in Rastafari

Worship in Rastafari is not about ritual for ritual's sake. It is rooted in a conscious awareness of the divine presence in all things. **"I and I"**, the central spiritual philosophy of

Rastafari, expresses the **oneness between the self and Jah**, and between all human beings. This concept permeates Rasta worship, which is both **individual and communal, meditative and expressive**, and always connected to the **natural order**.

Key elements of Rastafari worship include:

- **Daily prayer and meditation**;
- **Reading the Bible**, especially Psalms and prophetic books;
- **Reasoning sessions** (spiritual group discussions);
- **Chanting and singing Nyabinghi hymns**;
- **Drumming and music** as sacred expressions;
- **Observation of holy days and lunar cycles**.

---

1. Daily Prayer and Meditation

Rastafari practitioners often engage in **private prayer and meditation** multiple times a day. Prayer may not always follow a structured format, but it is sincere, focused, and aligned with scriptural principles. In place of memorized prayers, many Rastas speak **from the heart**, using language infused with reverence and self-awareness.

Common Themes in Rasta Prayer:

- Giving thanks to Jah for life, strength, and guidance;
- Seeking wisdom, clarity, and protection from evil;
- Offering prayers for family, the community, and the oppressed;
- Asking for deliverance from Babylon (systems of oppression);
- Maintaining spiritual focus while incarcerated.

Meditation may include **silent contemplation, chanting the Psalms**, or even **focused breathing** while repeating divine names such as "Jah Rastafari." This spiritual discipline helps maintain inner peace, especially in the often chaotic and violent prison environment.

2. Reading the Bible

The **Bible is a sacred text** in Rastafari, with particular emphasis on the **Old Testament**, the **Psalms**, and **prophetic books** such as Isaiah and Daniel. Rastas interpret the Bible through an **Afrocentric lens**, seeing it as a record of African people and their struggles, not a Eurocentric or colonial text.

Spiritual Focus in Rasta Biblical Study:

- **Psalms** are used daily for worship, healing, and protection.
- **Prophetic books** are read for understanding modern oppression and spiritual awakening.
- **Revelation and Daniel** are studied for their apocalyptic insights into Babylon.
- Scriptures about **Zion, Ethiopia**, and **liberation** are central to Rastafari theology.

Inmates often request access to **King James Version Bibles**, along with supplementary Rastafari literature that includes commentary, interpretations, and teachings of leaders like **Marcus Garvey, Haile Selassie I**, and **Leonard Howell**.

3. Reasoning Sessions

A **reasoning session** is a sacred gathering where Rastas come together to **discuss spiritual truths**, reflect on scripture, and elevate their collective consciousness. It is not a debate, but a peaceful and respectful exchange of insight.

These gatherings are often accompanied by prayer, chanting, and moments of silence. In correctional institutions, Rasta inmates often request access to shared spaces for reasoning — even in small groups. Reasoning is deeply rehabilitative, providing a space for:

- **Spiritual growth**;
- **Emotional support**;
- **Conflict resolution**;
- **Moral and ethical reflection**.

4. Chanting and Nyabinghi Worship

Nyabinghi is the spiritual heartbeat of Rastafari. It refers to a form of worship that includes **chanting, singing, drumming**, and deep prayer. Nyabinghi ceremonies often last several hours or even days, especially during major holy days or times of spiritual significance.

Elements of Nyabinghi Worship:

- **Drumming rhythms** that symbolize heartbeat, time, and ancestral presence;
- **Chanting the Psalms** and divine names;
- Singing **hymns of praise and liberation**;
- **Dancing and movement** in rhythm with the drumming.

Nyabinghi is both prayer and protest — a declaration of Jah's sovereignty and Babylon's fall. Though correctional institutions typically restrict instruments like drums, accommodations can still be made by allowing access to **recorded Nyabinghi chants, clapping, group singing**, or **chant circles** led by inmates themselves.

5. Observance of Holy Days and the Moon Cycle

Rastas observe a number of **sacred days**, including:

- **Haile Selassie's birthday** (July 23)
- **His coronation** (November 2)
- **Marcus Garvey's birthday** (August 17)
- **Grounation Day** (April 21)
- **The Ethiopian New Year** (Enkutatash – around September 11)

Some also observe **Sabbath** on Saturdays, avoiding labor and dedicating the day to rest, prayer, and scripture.

Additionally, some Rastafari follow **lunar cycles**, using the moon to guide periods of fasting, prayer, and reflection. Though practices vary, these observances carry deep **spiritual importance** and should be **recognized and accommodated** within correctional institutions.

Worship in Correctional Settings: Challenges and Solutions

Common Challenges:

- **No formal recognition** of Rastafari religious services;
- **Lack of space** for group worship or reasoning sessions;
- **No access to drums or music** for Nyabinghi expression;
- **Restrictions on head coverings** during worship;
- **Limited spiritual support** from chaplains unfamiliar with Rastafari.

These issues often stem from a **lack of resources**, not hostility. When correctional staff misunderstand the nature of Rastafari worship, it leads to denial of basic spiritual rights.

Institutional Solutions and Best Practices

To support Rasta inmates in practicing their faith:

✅ Recognize Rastafari as a legitimate religious tradition

Include it in chaplaincy programs, policy frameworks, and religious calendars.

✅ Provide spaces for reasoning and group worship

This can be a shared chapel, a multipurpose room, or even a designated time in a common area.

✅ Allow access to spiritual materials

Bibles, Rasta literature, recorded Nyabinghi chants, and journals for spiritual writing.

✅ Respect head coverings

Permit tam, crown, or wrap during prayer, meditation, and religious gatherings.

✅ Train staff in cultural competency

Education reduces misunderstanding and helps foster respectful interactions.

Voices from Inside: The Power of Worship

"Even though I'm behind bars, Jah hears I prayer. I chant Psalm 23 and Psalm 121 every day. That's I way of staying free."

"When we come together to reason, it's like the walls disappear. We feel like lions again — not inmates."

These testimonies reveal the **soul-deep power** of worship in Rastafari. It is not about ritual or performance — it is about **healing, clarity,** and the **presence of Jah in every moment**.

Conclusion

Rastafari worship is an ever-present force in the lives of its practitioners, whether they are free or incarcerated. It requires no elaborate buildings or clergy, only a committed heart, a clear mind, and a reverent spirit. For inmates who walk the path of Rastafari, worship is their anchor — a way to maintain dignity, purpose, and spiritual strength in the most challenging circumstances.

Correctional institutions that understand and respect Rasta worship not only fulfill legal obligations — they nurture the **transformative power of faith**, offering true rehabilitation and humanization behind the walls.

---

*Chapter 6 is all about the **role and symbolism of head coverings** in the Rastafari faith — a deeply sacred practice that is often misunderstood in correctional institutions. This chapter will explore the spiritual meaning behind crowns, tams, turbans, and other forms of headwear, along with guidance for institutional staff on why and how to **respect and accommodate this key religious expression**.*

📖 Chapter 6: The Role and Symbolism of Head Coverings in Rastafari

Introduction

In Rastafari, **head coverings are sacred garments**. They are not fashion accessories or personal style choices — they are **spiritual armor, crowns of dignity**, and **symbols of divine connection**. Worn by both men and women, head coverings serve as visible expressions of holiness, modesty, self-respect, and separation from Babylon (the corrupt world system).

Among the many aspects of the Rastafari faith, head coverings are **one of the most outwardly visible signs of spiritual commitment**, and often the most **contested or misunderstood** in correctional settings. When inmates are ordered to remove these coverings — for photographs, identification, searches, or disciplinary measures — they are often being asked to violate a **deeply held spiritual covenant**.

This chapter will unpack the **origins, meanings**, and **daily significance** of Rasta headwear, while offering practical solutions for institutions to **balance security needs with religious respect**.

Spiritual Significance of Head Coverings

1. Crown of Kings and Queens

Rastafari teaches that every man is a **king** and every woman is a **queen**, descendants of a royal African lineage that predates slavery and colonialism. Wearing a **crown**, **turban**, or **tam** is an expression of that spiritual royalty. The covering represents **divine authority**, **dignity**, and **self-mastery**.

"Jah say I-man is royalty. I don't remove I crown for Babylon. Not ever."

This symbolism is reinforced by the reverence for **Haile Selassie I**, the crowned Emperor of Ethiopia and living God in Rastafari belief. By wearing their own crowns, Rastas affirm their connection to a **divine royal heritage** — a counter to the dehumanization historically imposed on African people.

---

2. Covering the Crown Chakra

In Rasta spirituality, the **head is sacred**, as it is the seat of divine energy. Many adherents relate the head to the **crown chakra**, the energy center associated with spiritual connection, divine insight, and purity. Covering the head protects this energy and maintains spiritual alignment with Jah.

This belief is also echoed in other faith traditions — such as Sikhism, Islam, and Judaism — where head coverings symbolize **respect, humility, and spiritual focus**.

---

3. Modesty and Discipline

For Rasta women in particular, head wraps are a symbol of **modesty**, **self-respect**, and **spiritual discipline**. The practice of covering the head helps women remain centered, focused, and spiritually protected. It also reflects the **rejection of vanity and Babylonian ideals of beauty**, embracing instead the natural and divine.

Men also wear head coverings as an expression of **humility before Jah**, especially when praying, reading scripture, or participating in sacred reasoning sessions.

---

4. Protection of the Locks

Dreadlocks, which are a part of the **Nazirite vow** (see Chapter 3), are considered **sacred extensions of the spirit**. Covering them is an act of **protection, preservation**, and **reverence**. Many Rastas do not allow others to see, touch, or expose their locks in public or impure environments, especially where disrespect or hostility may be present — such as a correctional facility.

Forcing a Rasta to uncover their hair is akin to desecrating a temple — a serious spiritual offense.

Common Types of Rasta Head Coverings

1. **Tam or Rasta Crown**
   A round, knitted or sewn cap used to hold dreadlocks and cover the head. It may be colorful (often in red, gold, green, and black) or plain. The tam is the most widely worn head covering among male Rastas.
2. **Head Wrap / Turban (for Women and Men)**
   Long pieces of cloth wrapped elaborately around the head. Women often wear them as a symbol of modesty and spiritual focus, while some men wear turbans during worship or ceremonial gatherings.
3. **Scarf or Bandana**
   Used as a simple head covering for meditation, prayer, or daily wear when a full tam or wrap is unavailable.
4. **Ethiopian Crown / Priest's Turban**
   Worn by some Rastafari priests and elders, especially within the **Nyabinghi Order** or **Bobo Ashanti** house. These styles are often elaborate and worn only during formal ceremonies.

Head Coverings in Correctional Settings: The Conflict

In correctional institutions, especially those unfamiliar with Rastafari, **head coverings are often restricted or banned** under blanket policies aimed at preventing concealment of contraband, ensuring visual identification, or maintaining uniform appearance. These policies, while often security-based, can cause serious spiritual harm when they **fail to distinguish between religious items and personal attire**.

Common Institutional Policies:

- No hats or caps in housing units;
- Head coverings must be removed during ID photos, searches, or court appearances;

- Only authorized religious items allowed (often limited to Christianity, Islam, Judaism).

These rules often leave Rasta inmates in a painful dilemma: **obey institutional policy or remain true to their faith**. Refusing to remove a head covering can result in **disciplinary charges, segregation, or access restrictions**, despite constitutional rights to religious freedom.

Legal and Policy Protections in Canada

As covered in Chapter 2:

- **Section 2(a) of the Canadian Charter of Rights and Freedoms** guarantees freedom of religion;
- **Corrections and Conditional Release Act (CCRA)** mandates accommodation of spiritual practices unless safety is at risk;
- **CSC Commissioner's Directive 767** requires staff to consider the religious significance of head coverings and **not prohibit them arbitrarily**.

Any institutional rule that restricts head coverings must meet a **strict legal standard** of being justified, minimal, and necessary. Blanket bans — especially without consultation or review — may constitute a **Charter violation**.

Best Practices for Institutional Accommodation

To support the religious rights of Rastafari inmates while maintaining security, correctional institutions should consider the following:

✓ Allow Approved Religious Head Coverings

Tams, wraps, and turbans should be classified as **religious attire**, similar to kippahs (Judaism), hijabs (Islam), or turbans (Sikhism).

✓ Provide Clear Guidelines

Establish procedures that allow Rasta inmates to wear head coverings consistently, including during intake, worship, visitation, and daily life — not just during ceremonies.

✓ Educate Staff

Include Rastafari teachings on head coverings in cultural competency training, so staff can distinguish spiritual attire from gang symbolism or fashion.

✓ Respect During Searches and Photography

If a head covering must be removed for ID or security reasons, it should be done:

- **Privately** (not in front of others);
- **By staff of the same gender**;
- **With advance explanation and respect.**

✓ Avoid Disciplinary Action for Religious Practice

Refusing to remove a sacred head covering should not result in punishment if the action stems from **sincere religious belief**.

The Psychological and Spiritual Cost of Denial

When Rastafari inmates are forced to remove their head coverings, they may experience:

- **Spiritual distress** and disconnection from Jah;
- **Humiliation** and loss of dignity;
- **Anger, frustration, and emotional shutdown**;
- **Erosion of trust** in the correctional system;
- **Withdrawal from programs and group activities** to avoid compromising their faith.

Such outcomes **undermine rehabilitation**, damage mental health, and contribute to institutional conflict — all of which are preventable with informed policy and empathy.

Voices from Inside

"They told I to remove my crown for the photo. I told them this is not a hat — it's a sacred garment. But they didn't listen. I felt violated."

"When I wrap I locks, I feel protected. It's like putting on I spiritual armor. Without it, I feel exposed — like they can see inside I soul."

These testimonies show the **emotional and spiritual gravity** of head coverings in Rastafari. This is not rebellion — it is reverence.

Conclusion

For Rastafari adherents, head coverings are a sacred expression of **faith, identity, and divine authority**. They protect the spiritual center, honor African heritage, and represent a personal covenant with Jah. In correctional institutions, recognizing and accommodating these sacred garments is a matter of **constitutional right, religious respect, and human dignity**.

By creating space for Rastafari inmates to wear their crowns, tams, and wraps with pride, institutions affirm the possibility of **spiritual freedom behind bars** — and take a step toward truly rehabilitative, just, and inclusive correctional environments.

*Chapter 7, where we focus on **dreadlocks** — one of the most recognizable and deeply **spiritual expressions** of the Rastafari faith. This chapter will clarify their sacred purpose, dispel stereotypes, and explain why correctional institutions must **respect and protect** this profound religious commitment.*

📖 Chapter 7: Dreadlocks – A Spiritual Commitment, Not a Fashion Statement

Introduction

To the untrained eye, **dreadlocks** may appear to be a hairstyle — perhaps even a cultural trend or personal fashion choice. But for those who walk the path of Rastafari, dreadlocks are **sacred**. They are a visible, living testimony of the **Nazirite vow** (see Chapter 3), a covenant between the individual and **Jah (God)**. The growing, keeping, and never-cutting of the hair is not vanity — it is **spiritual discipline, ancestral reverence, and divine obedience**.

In correctional environments, where appearance is often heavily regulated, Rastafari inmates who wear dreadlocks frequently face **discrimination, disciplinary consequences**, or even **forced haircuts**. These actions are not only spiritually damaging — they may also violate **Canadian legal protections for religious freedom**.

This chapter explores the spiritual meaning of dreadlocks, the cultural and biblical roots of the practice, and the **urgent need** for informed, respectful policy in institutional settings.

The Origin of Dreadlocks in Rastafari

The keeping of dreadlocks is rooted in **scripture**, particularly in the **Old Testament**:

> "**All the days of the vow of his separation, no razor shall come upon his head: until the days be fulfilled, in the which he separateth himself unto the Lord, he shall be holy, and shall let the locks of the hair of his head grow.**"
> — Numbers 6:5 (KJV)

This is the **Nazirite vow**, a foundational pillar of Rastafari. By taking this vow, the Rasta chooses to:

- Separate from Babylon (worldly corruption);
- Dedicate themselves wholly to Jah;
- Let their hair grow naturally, untouched by razor or comb.

In this context, dreadlocks are not just long hair — they are **a spiritual covenant made visible**. Each lock tells a story of patience, discipline, and connection to the divine.

Symbolism of Dreadlocks in Rastafari

Dreadlocks carry **layers of spiritual, cultural, and political symbolism**, making them far more than a physical feature:

1. Spiritual Purity

Dreadlocks represent a life lived in **alignment with Jah**, free from vanity and worldliness. The hair is left to grow as nature intends — wild, free, and unmanipulated — symbolizing surrender to divine will.

2. Strength and Identity

Rastas often draw inspiration from the biblical figure **Samson**, whose strength was linked to his uncut hair. In the same way, dreadlocks are seen as a source of **spiritual power** and inner strength.

3. African Heritage and Resistance

Dreadlocks affirm **African identity** and resist Western beauty standards. They connect the wearer to their **roots**, both spiritually and ancestrally. During the era of slavery and colonization, African hair was stigmatized — Rastas reclaim it as a **crown of glory**.

4. Rejection of Babylon

In a world dominated by Babylonian systems — consumerism, oppression, racism — dreadlocks are an act of rebellion. They refuse to conform, refuse to be "cleaned up" for acceptance, and serve as a permanent mark of **spiritual resistance**.

Dreadlocks in the Correctional System: The Ongoing Struggle

Despite their sacred status, **dreadlocks are often misunderstood or targeted** in correctional settings. Common issues include:

◆ Grooming Policies

Many prisons enforce rules that require inmates to keep their hair "neat" or cut short, often citing hygiene or uniformity. Rastas who refuse to cut their dreadlocks on religious grounds may be labeled as noncompliant.

◆ Disciplinary Actions

Inmates have faced **disciplinary segregation**, denial of privileges, or program exclusion simply for maintaining their dreadlocks.

◆ Forced Haircuts

In some cases, dreadlocks have been forcibly cut during intake or disciplinary procedures — a traumatic and deeply **spiritually violating** act.

"When they cut I locks, they didn't just take hair — they took I soul. It felt like a funeral."
— Rastafari inmate, Ontario

◆ Stereotyping

Dreadlocks are frequently (and wrongly) associated with **gang affiliation**, drug culture, or defiance. These stereotypes lead to profiling, mockery, and exclusion — all of which **ignore the religious and cultural depth** of the practice.

Legal Protections in Canada

As addressed in previous chapters, the **Canadian Charter of Rights and Freedoms (Section 2a)** guarantees **freedom**

of religion, which includes expressions of faith such as dreadlocks.

Under the **Corrections and Conditional Release Act (CCRA)** and CSC policy (**Commissioner's Directive 767**), inmates are entitled to practice their religion **freely and openly**, as long as it does not interfere with institutional safety.

The Duty to Accommodate:

- Correctional institutions must **reasonably accommodate religious practices**, including the keeping of dreadlocks.
- If a grooming policy conflicts with a sincerely held religious belief, **exemptions must be made**, unless there is **a clear, demonstrable safety risk** — not just institutional convenience.

Courts and human rights tribunals in Canada have consistently ruled in favor of **religious accommodation**, especially when it comes to grooming and dress connected to identity and belief.

Best Practices for Institutions

✅ **Recognize Dreadlocks as a Religious Practice**

Treat dreadlocks in the same way you would treat **a Sikh turban, a Muslim hijab, or a Jewish yarmulke** — as sacred, not optional.

✅ **Adjust Grooming Policies**

Make room for religious exemptions that allow Rastas to keep their dreadlocks without facing discipline or exclusion.

✅ **Train Correctional Staff**

Educate officers and administrators about the **spiritual meaning** of dreadlocks, so they don't conflate them with gang affiliation or noncompliance.

✅ **Prohibit Forced Haircuts**

No one should be forced to violate their faith. If identification photos are needed, find **alternative procedures** that do not involve cutting hair.

✅ **Create Open Dialogue**

Allow Rasta inmates to meet with spiritual advisors or chaplains to discuss concerns related to their hair and grooming in a respectful, solutions-focused space.

Health and Hygiene Myths

A common myth in correctional institutions is that dreadlocks are **dirty or unclean**. This is a **false and culturally biased assumption**. In truth:

- Most Rastas are **highly hygienic**, washing their locks with natural products and taking pride in cleanliness.
- Dreadlocks are not unkempt — they are **naturally formed** and maintained through specific grooming routines.
- There is no evidence that dreadlocks pose a hygiene risk greater than any other hairstyle.

Banning dreadlocks on hygiene grounds is not only **unscientific**, but also a form of **cultural discrimination**.

Emotional and Spiritual Consequences

For a Rasta, the dreadlocks are **part of their soul**. Forcing their removal or mocking their appearance can lead to:

- **Spiritual trauma**;
- **Loss of religious identity**;
- **Withdrawal from rehabilitation programs**;
- **Increased tension and mistrust toward staff**;
- **Mental health deterioration** due to spiritual disconnection.

These outcomes are entirely preventable with **basic cultural respect and accommodation**.

Voices of the Faithful

"My locks are I sacrifice, I strength, I story. Each one is a testimony of survival, of love, of Jah."

"You wouldn't cut a Christian's cross off their neck. Don't cut I locks. They are not hair — they are I prayer."

These testimonies show that dreadlocks are **sacred acts of devotion**, not style statements.

Conclusion

Dreadlocks are far more than hair — they are **sacred extensions of spiritual purpose**, symbols of divine obedience, and deeply rooted connections to African identity and biblical faith. For Rastafari practitioners, especially those behind bars, their dreadlocks are often the **last thing they control** — the one unbroken covenant they still carry with Jah.

Correctional institutions that understand, protect, and accommodate dreadlocks are not just following the law — they are upholding the **basic dignity and humanity** of those in their care. Respect for dreadlocks is respect for faith, identity, and the transformative power of spirit.

*Chapter 8, where we explore the **language and communication styles** unique to the Rastafari faith. This is more than just vocabulary — it's a sacred linguistic rebellion against oppression and a spiritual elevation of everyday speech. In correctional settings, **understanding how Rastas speak** is key to avoiding miscommunication, disrespect, and mislabeling.*

Chapter 8: Rastafari Language and Communication Styles

Introduction

Language in Rastafari is a **powerful spiritual tool** — not just a means of communication, but a reflection of **identity, consciousness, and resistance**. Known as **"Iyaric"**, the Rastafari language system transforms colonial English into a dialect of liberation, positivity, and unity with the divine. It is rooted in **decolonization**, **Afrocentric thought**, and the belief that words hold power over the mind and spirit.

For those unfamiliar with it, Iyaric can be misunderstood as slang or improper English. In correctional settings, this misunderstanding can lead to **misinterpretation, disciplinary action**, or the unjust labeling of Rastafari inmates as disrespectful or noncompliant. But in truth, Rasta speech is **intentional, sacred, and philosophically rich**.

This chapter breaks down the core elements of Rasta language, its spiritual purpose, and how correctional staff can better **recognize and respect** this important part of the faith.

The Purpose of Rasta Language

Rastafari emerged in a colonial world where language was used as a **tool of oppression** — to strip Africans of their identity, control their narratives, and enforce submission. As a response, Rastas began **remaking English into a language of liberation**, removing oppressive structures and replacing them with affirmations of divinity, unity, and self-awareness.

The result is a spiritually charged dialect often referred to as **"Iyaric"**, "Dread Talk," or simply **Rasta speech**.

Rasta Language Serves Several Purposes:

- **Upliftment**: Replacing negative or dehumanizing words with ones that reflect divinity and positivity.
- **Spiritual Alignment**: Using Jah-centered language to stay in tune with divine presence.
- **Resistance**: Challenging the "Babylon" system by rejecting its language structures.
- **Unity**: Promoting "I and I" consciousness — the oneness of self and Jah, and of all people.

Key Features of Rasta Language

◆ 1. "I and I" – The Foundation of Unity

"I and I" is perhaps the most iconic Rasta phrase. It replaces "you and me" or "we" to **eliminate separation between the self, others, and Jah**.

"I and I give thanks."
(Meaning: We give thanks, united with Jah.)

This phrase reflects the belief that **Jah is within all**, and that true consciousness recognizes unity, not division.

◆ 2. Positive Rewording and Conscious Speech

Rastas avoid words they believe carry negative vibrations, colonial baggage, or spiritual poison. Instead, they reshape language to reflect truth, empowerment, and righteousness.

Examples:

Colonial English	Rasta Replacement	Reason
"Understand"	**"Overstand"**	Suggests a higher level of comprehension — not being "under" anything
"Hello"	**"Greetings"** or **"Blessed Love"**	"Hello" is seen to contain "hell"
"Oppress"	**"Downpress"**	More accurate — oppression pushes people down
"Subject"	**"Iject"** or **"Ijectivity"**	Avoids the connotation of submission
"Education"	**"Edification"**	Suggests enlightenment, not colonial schooling

The Rasta language is a living **affirmation of liberation**, built to **reclaim power** from Babylon and embed positivity into everyday life.

◆ 3. Phonetic Wordplay

Rasta language often reshapes words phonetically to **reflect truth or spiritual meaning**.

- **"Ises"** = Praises (used in worship)
- **"Ital"** = Vital (clean and pure, especially in diet)
- **"Livicate"** = Replace "dedicate" (which includes "dead") with a term meaning "give life to"

This restructuring not only defies Babylonian norms but also helps keep **spiritual awareness embedded in daily speech**.

◆ 4. Use of Ethiopian and Biblical Terms

Because of the sacred connection to Ethiopia and the Bible, many Rastas incorporate words from **Amharic** (Ethiopian language) and **biblical King James English**.

- **"Selah"** = A pause or affirmation in prayer or scripture.
- **"Ras"** = A title meaning "prince" or "head" in Amharic (e.g., Ras Tafari).
- **"Negus"** = King, often referring to Haile Selassie I.
- **"Zion"** = Holy land or divine state of being.
- **"Babylon"** = System of oppression, prison, or corrupt society.

Communication Styles: Calm, Reasoned, and Reverent

Rastafari communication is often **calm, deliberate, and respectful**, especially during spiritual discussions known as **reasoning**. These sessions are based on:

- **Mutual respect**;

- **Deep listening**;
- **Non-confrontational truth-sharing**;
- **Centering Jah in all things**.

In correctional facilities, Rasta inmates may request time and space for reasoning, much like a prayer circle or Bible study in other traditions. These are **not gang meetings** or casual hangouts — they are sacred dialogues intended to **elevate consciousness**.

Misinterpretations in Correctional Settings

1. Mislabeling Speech as "Defiance"

Because Rasta speech avoids colonial language, a Rasta might choose not to say "Sir" or "Yes, ma'am." Instead, they may respond with:

"I overstand, bredren."
or
"Blessed love, officer."

This is not disrespect — it's a **sincere form of communication**, rooted in their worldview. Misreading this as defiance is a failure of cultural understanding.

2. Language Barriers with Staff

Staff unfamiliar with Iyaric may find it difficult to interpret Rasta speech, especially if metaphors or biblical references are used. What may sound like coded language or evasion is often **spiritual metaphor or poetic reasoning**.

"I walk not inna Babylon's shadow, for Jah light up I path."

(Translation: I don't follow corrupt ways; I follow divine truth.)

3. Mockery or Disrespect

Due to media stereotypes, some officers or fellow inmates may **mock Rasta speech** — treating it like a joke, impression, or slang. This is **deeply offensive** and contributes to spiritual isolation.

Legal and Ethical Responsibilities

In Canada, **Section 2(a) of the Charter** and **CSC directives** protect an inmate's right to express their faith **in language and practice**. That includes:

- Speaking in Iyaric;
- Using spiritual greetings;
- Participating in reasoning sessions;
- Having access to spiritual materials written in Rasta language.

Failure to respect these rights could be considered **religious discrimination**, especially if it leads to punitive action or exclusion from programs.

Recommendations for Correctional Institutions

✓ **Train Staff in Rasta Communication**

Basic familiarity with Rasta terms, greetings, and speech patterns can prevent miscommunication and reduce conflict.

✅ Don't Dismiss Rasta Language as Slang

Recognize Iyaric as a form of **sacred expression**, not broken English.

✅ Allow Reasoning Sessions and Spiritual Dialogue

These gatherings support mental clarity, community building, and spiritual growth.

✅ Support Literacy in Rasta Teachings

Make books, dictionaries, and spiritual materials available that reflect Rasta language and worldview.

✅ Encourage Cultural Humility

If an officer doesn't understand a phrase, they can respectfully ask, "Can you help me understand what that means in your faith?"

Voices from the Inside

"Words are power. Babylon use words to break I spirit. But I use I words to rise."

"Rasta talk is prayer, not slang. Every 'I' is Jah inside I soul."

These words reflect the depth and holiness of Rastafari communication — a system of **self-liberation through language**.

Conclusion

Rastafari language is a sacred rhythm of truth, resistance, and reverence. Every phrase, every substitution, is a deliberate act of **decolonization and spiritual empowerment**. In correctional settings, this language becomes a shield, a compass, and a voice for dignity — one that should be **respected, not punished**.

By embracing the beauty and wisdom of Rasta communication, institutions can take one more step toward **inclusive rehabilitation**, cultural understanding, and human rights.

*Chapter 9, where we explore the **natural heart of the Rastafari faith** — the sacred relationship with **nature, herbs, and holistic healing**. In a world dominated by pharmaceuticals and industrial health systems, Rastas return to **creation as the source of healing**, aligning the body, mind, and spirit with the Earth and the **divine will of Jah**.*

📖 Chapter 9: The Importance of Nature, Herbal Use, and Holistic Healing in Rastafari

Introduction

At the root of the Rastafari faith is a **deep reverence for nature**. Rastafari teaches that **creation is divine**, that the Earth is not something to be exploited, but to be honored, preserved, and lived in harmony with. From the foods Rastas eat (Ital), to the air they breathe, to the plants they use for healing and meditation, everything in nature is seen as **a direct expression of Jah**.

For the Rastafari, **health is spiritual**. The body is a **temple**, and to heal it is to **restore balance with nature and Jah**. This belief stands in sharp contrast to Babylon's systems of medicine, which are often viewed as **unnatural, chemical-heavy, and spiritually detached**. In correctional environments, where institutional healthcare often favors pharmaceuticals over plant-based remedies, this worldview is **frequently ignored or disrespected**.

This chapter explores how Rastafari engages with nature and healing, the role of herbs like **ganja**, and what correctional institutions need to understand about **natural medicine as sacred practice**.

Livity: Living in Harmony with Nature

The concept of **"livity"** — a core Rastafari principle — refers to **living in accordance with divine life energy**. That energy flows through all living things: the trees, the rivers, the animals, the sun, the soil, and especially within the **human body**.

Rasta teachings on livity include:

- Eating only natural foods (Ital);
- Avoiding synthetic drugs, alcohol, and chemicals;
- Breathing clean air and spending time in nature;
- Using **herbs and plants** for healing and spiritual clarity;
- Treating the Earth with **respect and stewardship**.

Living naturally is not optional — it is a **spiritual commandment**. To be disconnected from nature is to be disconnected from **Jah**.

"The earth is Jah garden. Everything we need for healing, Him already plant."

Herbalism in Rastafari: Sacred and Medicinal

Herbs are central to the **Rastafari approach to healing**. They are not only medicine, but also **sacrament, prayer, and ancestral wisdom**. The use of herbs is both practical and spiritual — a way to cleanse the body, calm the mind, and elevate the soul.

Commonly used herbs in Rastafari tradition:

- **Ganja (Cannabis sativa)** – Used for meditation, healing, and reasoning;
- **Sarsaparilla** – Blood cleanser, high in iron;
- **Guinea Hen Weed (Anamu)** – Boosts immunity, anti-inflammatory;
- **Cerasse (Bitter Bush)** – Detoxifier and liver cleanser;

- **Lemongrass** – Used for digestion, fever, and spiritual baths;
- **Mint, ginger, and turmeric** – For calming the stomach, inflammation, and circulation.

Herbs are typically used in the form of **teas, steams, poultices, baths, or inhalation**, depending on the ailment or spiritual intent.

Ganja: The Most Misunderstood Herb

No discussion of Rastafari healing is complete without **ganja**, the most sacred and most **misrepresented** herb in the faith.

What Ganja Is in Rastafari:

- A **sacrament** used to open the mind to meditation;
- A **spiritual key** to deepen reasoning sessions and connect with Jah;
- A **healing herb** that brings peace to the body and clarity to the soul;
- A **natural alternative** to synthetic drugs for treating anxiety, insomnia, and pain.

Rastas do not view ganja as a recreational drug. Its use is **ceremonial, spiritual, and guided by discipline**. It is never used to escape reality, but to **confront it with divine insight**.

"When I blaze di herb, I no run from Babylon. I see it clear. I see Jah plan. I overstand life."

The Babylonian View

Despite its sacred role, ganja has been criminalized and stigmatized globally — often used as a tool to persecute and marginalize Rastas. This includes within correctional systems, where Rastas are often denied access to spiritual practice involving ganja and may face **stigma or suspicion** just for speaking about it.

Though **legal in Canada under certain conditions**, ganja is still **prohibited in correctional institutions**. While Rastas generally understand these legal restrictions, institutions must be careful not to **equate the desire for ganja with criminal intent**. Instead, they should acknowledge:

- The **spiritual importance** of the herb;
- The **philosophical beliefs** behind its use;
- The need for **respectful alternatives** for meditation and healing when ganja is inaccessible.

The Body as Temple

Rastafari teaches that the **body is a vessel of Jah**. It must be kept clean, pure, and strong in order to carry out divine work. Therefore, Rastas **resist vaccinations, injections, painkillers, and synthetic drugs**, especially when alternatives exist.

This can create conflict in prisons, where medical care is often limited to **conventional Western approaches**. When Rasta inmates refuse pills or request herbal treatments, they may be labeled as:

- Noncompliant;
- Delusional;
- Disruptive;
- Manipulative.

But in truth, this resistance comes from a place of **faith and spiritual integrity**. It is a **religious practice**, not a behavioral issue.

Nature and Healing in Prison: Challenges

Correctional environments are, by design, unnatural spaces. Concrete, fluorescent lighting, poor air circulation, processed food, and lack of access to green space all work against the Rastafari ideal of **livity**.

Major barriers include:

- **No access to herbs or natural remedies**;
- **Over-reliance on pills** for physical and mental health;
- **Isolation from sunlight, fresh air, and soil**;
- **No spiritual use of ganja**, even in small, sacred amounts;
- **Lack of chaplaincy support** for natural medicine and holistic healing.

These conditions can lead to **spiritual sickness** in Rastafari inmates — a deep sense of disconnection from Jah and creation.

Legal and Ethical Considerations

The **Canadian Charter of Rights and Freedoms**, along with **CSC directives**, require that correctional institutions **accommodate religious practices**. While they are not obligated to provide ganja or every herbal request, they are **required to show respect and flexibility** in:

- Dietary accommodations (Ital);
- Allowing inmates to possess herbal books and writings;
- Supporting non-invasive, natural alternatives when possible;
- Acknowledging the **religious and cultural importance of herbs**.

Best Practices for Institutions

✅ Educate Healthcare and Security Staff

Help them understand that herbal knowledge is not pseudoscience or manipulation — it's spiritual medicine.

✅ Support Access to Natural Options

Within policy, allow inmates access to **herbal teas, non-caffeinated drinks, and natural foods** that support their health philosophy.

✅ Provide Books and Study Materials

Allow inmates to access **Rasta herbal guides**, natural healing texts, and related literature.

✅ Respect Refusal of Medication

If a Rasta inmate declines medication, do not assume noncompliance. Instead, consult a spiritual advisor or chaplain.

✅ Allow Outdoor Time and Sunlight

Time outside is vital to **Rasta well-being**, even if only for a few minutes a day.

Voices from the Faithful

"Babylon try give I pill for what the bush can fix. I no trust it. Jah plant every remedy already."

"I don't want the medicine that dull I soul. Give I the earth — the root, the steam, the tea. That is I healing."

These voices remind us that **healing is not one-size-fits-all** — and that spiritual paths must be respected, even in confinement.

Conclusion

To walk the Rastafari path is to walk **in rhythm with the Earth and the Most High**. Nature is not just scenery — it is the **temple of Jah**, and within it lies everything needed for healing, clarity, and connection. Herbs are not drugs. They are **divine tools**, rooted in ancient wisdom and spiritual purpose.

Correctional institutions that recognize this — that open space for holistic healing, natural living, and cultural respect — are not just managing inmates. They are creating an environment where **faith, dignity, and true rehabilitation can grow**.

*Chapter 10, where we reason on the **Biblical roots of the Rastafari faith**. Though often dismissed or misunderstood by outsiders, the Rastafari movement is **deeply scriptural**, grounded in the **Old Testament**, the **Psalms**, and **prophetic texts** that speak directly to liberation, divine kingship, and African identity. Let's overstand how the **Holy Bible** is not only a spiritual guide for Rastas, but also a **source of prophecy, justice, and resistance**.*

📖 Chapter 10: Rastafari and the Bible – Scriptural Foundations of the Faith

Introduction

Contrary to popular misconceptions, Rastafari is a **Bible-based faith**. The scriptures — especially the **King James Version** — are seen as sacred, containing the words and prophecies of **Jah Almighty**. The Bible is not read passively; it is **interpreted through the lens of African consciousness**, with a focus on justice, divine rulership, and the fulfillment of prophecy through **Emperor Haile Selassie I**, the Lion of Judah.

For many Rastas, the Bible reveals the **true history of Black people**, and it serves as a **spiritual compass** in a world corrupted by Babylon. In correctional environments, where faith becomes a source of inner strength, the Bible plays a central role in **daily worship, meditation, and survival**.

In this chapter, we explore the **key scriptures, prophetic links**, and the **unique Rasta interpretation** of the Bible — as well as how correctional systems can better **respect and support access** to this sacred text.

The King James Version: The Chosen Text

Most Rastas use the **King James Version (KJV)** of the Bible. It is preferred for its poetic structure, its closeness to ancient language, and its use by **Marcus Garvey**, who is considered a **prophet** in the faith.

While some Rastafari also study texts like the **Book of Enoch**, the **Kebra Nagast** (a 14th-century Ethiopian manuscript), or the **Apocrypha**, the KJV remains the **core spiritual guide**. Rastas do not rely on church interpretations — instead, they read the Bible with **spiritual insight**, guided by meditation, intuition, and the **Irits (spirit)**.

"The Bible is no Babylon book. It is Jah word, but you must read it with open I."

Key Biblical Themes in Rastafari

◆ 1. Zion and Babylon

This is one of the central dualities in Rasta theology.

- **Zion** represents **Ethiopia**, Africa, righteousness, divine order, and spiritual homeland.
- **Babylon** represents **oppression**, colonization, the West, corruption, and false systems of control.

Psalm 137:1
"By the rivers of Babylon, there we sat down, yea, we wept, when we remembered Zion."

This verse is chanted, sung, and reasoned upon regularly in Rastafari, especially in prison — where Babylon's grip is most literal. It speaks to both **physical exile** and **spiritual longing** for liberation.

◆ 2. The Promised King: Haile Selassie I

Rastas see the Bible as foretelling the rise of a **divine African king** — a role fulfilled by **Emperor Haile Selassie I** of Ethiopia. Several scriptures are seen as **prophecies** of his reign:

Revelation 5:5
"Behold, the Lion of the tribe of Judah, the Root of David, hath prevailed..."

Psalm 68:31
"Princes shall come out of Egypt; Ethiopia shall soon stretch out her hands unto God."

Genesis 49:10
"The sceptre shall not depart from Judah..."

Haile Selassie, born **Ras Tafari Makonnen**, is believed to be the **living God**, the **King of Kings**, and the **conquering Lion of Judah** — titles he held officially in Ethiopian coronation.

◆ 3. Liberation and Deliverance

The Bible's liberation narrative — particularly the story of **Moses and the Exodus** — resonates deeply with Rastafari, mirroring the **Black struggle** against slavery, colonization, and racial injustice.

Exodus 3:7–8
"I have surely seen the affliction of my people... and I am come down to deliver them."

This story is not viewed as ancient history, but as **living prophecy** for African people globally — especially those still locked behind Babylon's bars.

◆ 4. The Nazirite Vow and Dreadlocks

As explored in Chapter 3, Rastafari's commitment to dreadlocks and spiritual purity is grounded in:

Numbers 6:5
"There shall no razor come upon his head: until the days be fulfilled, in the which he separateth himself unto the Lord..."

This vow is lived daily through dreadlocks, Ital diet, and abstinence from defilement — forming the **core of Rasta spiritual discipline**.

◆ 5. Psalms as Daily Prayer and Chant

Rastas turn to the **Psalms** for comfort, guidance, and power. These sacred songs are chanted during Nyabinghi gatherings, private prayer, and group worship.

Popular Psalms in Rasta Worship:

- **Psalm 1** – The righteous path;
- **Psalm 23** – Jah is I shepherd;
- **Psalm 27** – Jah is I light and salvation;
- **Psalm 121** – I will lift up mine eyes;
- **Psalm 137** – Lament of exile and Babylon;
- **Psalm 68** – Procession of the Most High.

Psalms are often **spoken rhythmically**, sometimes with drumming, forming the **heartbeat of Rasta spiritual life** — especially in prison, where music and song are limited.

Rasta Interpretation of the Bible

Unlike mainstream Christian traditions that often interpret the Bible through institutional theology, Rastafari emphasizes **direct personal revelation**.

Rasta Reading of Scripture Includes:

- **Afrocentric interpretation** — understanding Biblical people as African, including Christ, Moses, Solomon, and David;
- **Symbolic and mystical meanings** — viewing stories as ongoing spiritual realities;
- **Critique of Babylonian religion** — rejecting the colonial church that used scripture to oppress.

Rastas hold that **Jah lives within**, and therefore, **each person can discern truth** from scripture through meditation, overstanding, and Iritual guidance.

The Bible Behind Bars

In correctional institutions, the Bible becomes even more vital. For Rasta inmates, it is:

- A **source of daily discipline**;
- A **way to maintain livity**;
- A **channel of communication with Jah**;
- A tool for **meditation, growth, and focus**.

However, some correctional systems fail to recognize how differently Rastas use and interpret the Bible, leading to:

- Mislabeling their beliefs as non-Christian or illegitimate;
- Denying access to related sacred texts (Kebra Nagast, Rasta commentaries);
- Excluding them from Christian services that don't align with their doctrine.

Legal and Institutional Responsibility

Correctional institutions in Canada are obligated under the **Charter of Rights and Freedoms** and the **Corrections and Conditional Release Act** to:

- Provide access to religious texts;
- Allow group study and scripture-based gatherings;
- Respect differing interpretations of scripture;
- Permit Rasta chaplains or advisors to guide inmates.

Limiting access to the Bible or punishing its unique interpretation would be a **violation of religious rights**.

Best Practices for Correctional Institutions

✅ Provide Access to the King James Bible

Ensure Rastafari inmates can receive personal or institutional copies.

✅ Permit Supplemental Sacred Texts

Include texts like the **Kebra Nagast**, **Rasta Bible interpretations**, and **Garvey's speeches** where possible.

✅ Allow Psalm Chanting and Group Reading

Support safe, structured group worship rooted in scripture.

✅ Educate Chaplains on Rasta Theology

Help chaplains understand the unique way Rastas approach scripture and avoid imposing conflicting doctrines.

Voices of the Faithful

"The Bible is I shield. Babylon try break I body, but the Word keep I strong."

"Psalm 23 is I morning bread. Psalm 27 is I warrior chant. Every verse, a piece of freedom."

Conclusion

The **Holy Bible is central to the Rastafari faith** — not as a static book of rules, but as a **living map to divine overstanding, liberation, and prophecy**. For Rastas, it confirms that their identity, struggle, and destiny are **scripturally rooted and spiritually valid**.

In the correctional system, where spiritual survival becomes a daily battle, the Bible offers **light in darkness**, structure in chaos, and connection in confinement. Respecting that relationship is not just a legal duty — it is a recognition of the **sacred power of the Word**, and its ability to transform lives, even behind concrete walls.

Chapter 11, bringing in the **sound and power** of Rastafari through the sacred elements of **music, chanting, and vibration**. In Rasta livity, music isn't just for entertainment — it is **spiritual warfare, prayer in rhythm**, and a **sacred tool for reasoning and healing**. Let's chant down Babylon proper in this one.

📖 Chapter 11: Music and Chanting in Rastafari Worship

Introduction

"**Chant down Babylon**" — this isn't just a lyric. It's a spiritual command.

In the Rastafari faith, **music and chanting are sacred practices** used to invoke the presence of Jah, purify the atmosphere, and unite the brethren and sistren in spirit. These are not casual performances or shows; they are **acts of devotion**, **resistance**, and **communication with the Most High**.

Rooted in **ancient African traditions, Hebrew psalms,** and **Ethiopian Orthodox rhythms**, Rastafari music is a weapon of spiritual warfare — uplifting the righteous and shaking the foundations of Babylon.

This chapter explores the divine role of music in Rasta worship, with a focus on **Nyabinghi chanting**, **reggae as a ministry**, and the healing power of rhythm — especially within correctional settings, where that rhythm becomes a lifeline of faith and freedom.

The Sacred Role of Music in Rastafari

In Rastafari, music is **livity made audible**. It is the **voice of the Irits**, the spiritual breath of Jah moving through word, sound, and power. Music isn't separate from worship — **it is worship**.

It serves multiple sacred purposes:

- **Praises to the Most High** (Jah);
- **Chanting scripture**, especially Psalms;
- **Resistance against oppression** (chanting down Babylon);
- **Healing the mind and body**;
- **Bringing the community together** in one heart and one aim.

"Word, sound, and power — this is the trinity of I worship. When I chant, I don't just sing. I speak prophecy."

Nyabinghi Chanting: The Heartbeat of Rasta Worship

Nyabinghi is the original spiritual order of Rastafari. Its name comes from an ancient East African queen and later came to signify **the order of warriors, healers, and priests** within Rasta livity. At the center of Nyabinghi worship is **chanting and drumming**.

What Happens in a Nyabinghi Gathering:

- **Drumming** using three sacred drums: the **bass**, the **fundeh**, and the **repeater** (akete);
- **Chanting of Psalms and sacred songs**;
- **Prayer, reasoning, and meditation**;
- **Movement and dancing** in unity;
- Burning of **frankincense, myrrh**, and sometimes **herb** to sanctify the space.

These gatherings can last all night — even for days — especially during holy celebrations like **Grounation Day, Coronation Day**, or **Haile Selassie's Earthstrong** (birthday).

The Nyabinghi Drums: Word, Sound, and Power

1. **The Bass Drum**
   - Keeps the foundation. The **heartbeat of creation**.
   - Played with a soft mallet in a slow, steady pulse.
2. **The Fundeh Drum**
   - Plays the **time** — a steady, syncopated rhythm that holds balance.
   - Keeps the chant grounded.
3. **The Repeater (Akete) Drum**
   - The voice of the Irits. Improvises and speaks to the soul.
   - Carries the **prophetic vibration**, often played with intensity during high spiritual moments.

"When di repeater call out, I heart answer. Is like Jah talking through sound."

Chanting as Worship and Resistance

The chants sung in Nyabinghi worship are drawn from:

- **Biblical Psalms and scriptures**;
- **African spiritual melodies**;
- **Original Rasta hymns**, passed down through generations;
- **Improvised spiritual utterances**, led by the drumming.

Common themes include:

- Praises to Jah;
- Deliverance from Babylon;
- Unity and peace among the people;

- Honoring of Ethiopian heritage;
- Reflection on righteousness, Zion, and overstanding.

Chants may be sung in English, **broken patois**, or **Amharic** — depending on the house and gathering.

Reggae Music: The Ministry of Word, Sound, and Power

While Nyabinghi chanting is the spiritual core, **reggae** became the **global voice of Rastafari**. Artists like **Bob Marley, Peter Tosh, Burning Spear, Midnite, Ijahman Levi**, and many more turned the teachings of Rasta into melodies that reached **the four corners of the earth**.

Reggae is used to:

- Spread the message of **Jah, love, justice, and repatriation**;
- **Expose corruption**, injustice, and colonial oppression;
- Unite the African diaspora and all oppressed peoples;
- Serve as **spiritual encouragement** for those suffering or imprisoned.

Even within correctional institutions, reggae serves as **inspiration**, a way for inmates to maintain their connection to their roots, their faith, and their sense of identity.

"Marley teach more gospel than any preacher. His songs is sermon, every lyric a lesson."

Music in Correctional Settings: A Sacred Necessity

Music — especially chanting and drumming — is often **restricted or misunderstood** in correctional environments. Instruments may be banned, gatherings limited, and Rasta music dismissed as recreational or cultural instead of **religious**.

But for Rastafari inmates, music is not entertainment — it's **daily worship**, **spiritual medicine**, and a tool for **self-rehabilitation**.

Common Barriers Faced:

- **Drum bans**, even for religious ceremonies;
- **Misclassification of Rasta music as gang-related**;
- **Lack of access to spiritual recordings**;
- **No designated time or space for chanting or music worship**.

These restrictions cut off Rastas from a major aspect of their spiritual life, contributing to **spiritual distress** and **emotional isolation**.

Legal Considerations and Rights

In Canada, under:

- **Section 2(a) of the Charter of Rights and Freedoms** (freedom of religion),
- and the **Corrections and Conditional Release Act (CCRA)**,

Rastafari inmates have the right to **spiritual practice**, which includes:

- Chanting Psalms and Rasta hymns;

- Listening to spiritual music and reggae with religious content;
- Holding group worship with recorded drumming if live drums are not possible;
- Accessing religious music in libraries or personal devices, if available.

Best Practices for Institutions

✅ Recognize Chanting and Music as Religious Practice

Include Nyabinghi and Rasta worship in religious service offerings.

✅ Allow Recorded Drumming and Chants

If live drums aren't allowed, provide recordings for group or individual worship.

✅ Include Rasta Music in Chaplaincy and Cultural Programs

Songs by conscious Rasta artists should be recognized as **spiritual resources**.

✅ Support Music-Based Rehabilitation

Encourage songwriting, spiritual expression through rhythm, and faith-based music circles.

Voices from the Inside

"When I chant Psalms with my idren, it feel like Jah walk through the cell. The walls can't hold down that power."

"Reggae music keep I sane. When Babylon press I mind, the drum remind I who I am."

These words remind us: for Rasta inmates, **music is prayer**, **drumming is heartbeat**, and **chanting is survival**.

Conclusion

In the Rastafari faith, **music is not a background noise — it is the voice of Jah**. From Nyabinghi chants to conscious reggae, every beat, every lyric, every chant is a spiritual declaration of liberation, unity, and truth.

For incarcerated Rastas, this music carries them through dark nights, solitary days, and spiritual warfare. Correctional institutions must come to recognize this sacred practice not as noise, but as **vibration of life** — a bridge to healing, dignity, and divine connection.

Let the chant rise. Let the drum beat. **Let the walls of Babylon tremble**.

---

*Chapter 12, where we shine the light on the **sacred times and observances** in the Rastafari calendar. These holy days are not just celebrations — they are moments of **reflection, spiritual recharge, ancestral connection**, and **reaffirmation of livity**. In the correctional setting, understanding and respecting these days is **essential to honoring religious freedom**.*

📖 Chapter 12: Holy Days and Observances in the Rastafari Calendar

Introduction

In Rastafari, time is not just counted — it is **honored**. Sacred days in the Rasta calendar are **vibrational points**, deeply tied to prophecy, African history, and the movement of Jah's spirit. These observances commemorate **divine events, liberation struggles, earthstrongs (birthdays)** of prophets, and key moments in **Ethiopian and diasporic history**.

Each holy day is a chance to **realign with the Most High**, reconnect with the **community**, chant down Babylon, and **celebrate the rise of Black consciousness**. For Rastas, these dates are as sacred as Easter, Ramadan, or Yom Kippur are in other traditions.

Correctional institutions must **acknowledge and accommodate** these observances by allowing Rasta inmates time, space, and spiritual resources to participate in these holy rites.

The Most Important Holy Days in the Rastafari Calendar

◆ 1. Grounation Day – April 21

This is one of the most **sacred days in Rastafari livity**, commemorating the historic 1966 visit of **Emperor Haile Selassie I to Jamaica**. Seen as a **divine visitation**, the event marked the fulfillment of prophecy and solidified the Emperor's connection to the Rasta people.

On this day, thousands gathered at the airport in Kingston to welcome His Imperial Majesty. Rain fell. Then the sun appeared as the Lion of Judah stepped from the plane. The land trembled in spiritual recognition.

Rasta Observance Includes:

- Nyabinghi drumming and chanting;
- Scripture reading and reasoning;
- Prayer, fasting, and purification;
- Celebrations of unity and liberation.

◆ 2. Coronation Day – November 2

This day celebrates the **coronation of Ras Tafari as Emperor Haile Selassie I in 1930**, when he received titles like *King of Kings, Lord of Lords, Conquering Lion of Judah*, and *Elect of God*. This event is seen as the **fulfillment of Revelation 5:5** and a confirmation of his divinity.

Rasta Observance Includes:

- Reading Psalms and scriptures like Revelation;
- Wearing ceremonial white or Ethiopian colors;
- Chanting praises to the Most High;
- Reaffirming personal commitment to livity and the Nazirite vow.

◆ 3. Haile Selassie I Earthstrong (Birthday) – July 23

This marks the **birth of Emperor Haile Selassie I in 1892**. It is both a celebration of life and a renewal of devotion to his example of **dignity, wisdom, and justice**.

Observed with:

- Nyabinghi worship;
- Fasting or Ital feasting;
- Testimonies and readings about His Majesty's life;
- Reflection on African kingship and divine leadership.

◆ 4. Marcus Garvey Earthstrong – August 17

Prophet **Marcus Mosiah Garvey**, born in 1887, is honored as the **forerunner of the faith**, the one who proclaimed, *"Look to Africa for the crowning of a Black king."* That prophecy is seen as foretelling Haile Selassie's rise.

Garvey represents:

- Black empowerment;
- Pan-African vision;
- Repatriation and mental liberation;
- Rasta roots in resistance and self-determination.

Rasta Observance Includes:

- Public speeches and readings of Garvey's teachings;
- Celebrations of African heritage;
- Acts of service or education;
- Meditation on repatriation and liberation.

◆ 5. Ethiopian New Year – Enkutatash (around September 11)

Rastafari observes the **Ethiopian calendar**, which celebrates New Year in September. This is a time for **spiritual renewal**, cleansing, and planting new intentions for the coming year.

Observed with:

- Fasting or Ital feasts;
- Reading the Psalms;
- Spiritual baths or meditation;
- Chanting and thanksgiving to Jah.

◆ 6. Redemption Day – August 1

Also known as **Emancipation Day** in many parts of the Caribbean, this day marks the **abolition of slavery** in British colonies in 1834. For Rastas, it is a day of **deep reflection on physical and mental slavery**, and a call to complete **spiritual emancipation**.

"None but ourselves can free our minds." – Bob Marley (inspired by Garvey)

◆ 7. Sabbath – Every Saturday

Many Rastas observe the **Sabbath on Saturday**, in alignment with the **Ethiopian Orthodox Church** and certain Biblical traditions.

Rasta Sabbath Includes:

- Rest from labor;
- Scripture study;
- Ital meals or fasting;
- Silent meditation or group reasoning.

In prison, allowing Rastas to observe the Sabbath respectfully is as important as Friday prayers for Muslims or Sunday worship for Christians.

Rituals and Practices Associated with Holy Days

On these sacred days, Rastas may engage in:

- **Fasting** (abstaining from food, speaking, or negative energy);
- **Nyabinghi ceremonies**;
- **Ritual cleansing** with water or herbs;
- **Scripture reading**, especially Psalms and prophetic books;
- **Wearing of spiritual garments** (white, red/gold/green, Ethiopian emblems);
- **Burning of incense** (if permitted) or diffusing spiritual scents;
- **Lighting of candles** for prayer or reasoning.

These are not "optional" activities. They are **essential expressions of faith**, tied to the **soul's alignment with Jah**.

Challenges in Correctional Environments

Despite the sacred nature of these days, Rasta inmates often face:

- Denial of time to gather or worship;
- Restrictions on head coverings or clothing;
- Lack of access to special Ital meals or fasting accommodations;
- Dismissal of Rasta holy days as non-legitimate holidays;
- Conflicts with scheduled work or institutional duties.

These challenges **violate religious rights** and hinder the spiritual development of the individual.

Legal Support in Canada

As outlined in earlier chapters:

- **Section 2(a) of the Canadian Charter** protects the right to religious observance;
- The **Corrections and Conditional Release Act (CCRA)** affirms inmates' rights to spiritual practice;
- **CSC Commissioner's Directive 767** mandates that all recognized religious holidays must be **respected and reasonably accommodated**, including those from minority faiths like Rastafari.

Best Practices for Institutions

✅ Include Rastafari Holy Days in Religious Calendars

Ensure chaplaincy and staff are aware of dates and their significance.

✅ Allow Group Worship or Observance

Permit small gatherings, even if modest — chanting, prayer, or scripture reading.

✅ Accommodate Special Meals or Fasting

Work with dietary staff to ensure Ital or fasting-compatible options are provided.

✅ **Train Staff on Cultural Sensitivity**

Help correctional officers understand that these days carry **deep spiritual meaning**.

✅ **Document Accommodation Procedures**

Inmates should have a clear and respectful way to request holy day observance.

Voices of the Faithful

"Grounation Day remind I that Jah walk among I people. Even behind bars, I chant to honor that moment."

"When the system don't recognize Rasta holy days, it's like saying I faith don't exist. But Jah know. I still praise."

These reflections show that **sacred time is spiritual oxygen**. Denying it is not just administrative oversight — it is spiritual harm.

Conclusion

The holy days of the Rastafari calendar are not mere traditions — they are **sacred portals in time**, deeply tied to prophecy, spiritual awakening, and historical truth. For Rasta practitioners, especially those incarcerated, these observances are a vital part of **spiritual health, identity, and resilience**.

Correctional institutions that **acknowledge and accommodate** these days do more than follow the law — they uphold **human dignity, religious freedom**, and the right to worship in spirit and in truth.

Chapter 13, *where we reason 'pon the **real-world discrimination faced by Rastafari**, both in correctional institutions and broader society. This chapter shines a light on the **legal rights**, **constitutional protections**, and the need for **spiritual justice** — especially for Rasta bredren and sistren held within Babylon's walls.*

📖 Chapter 13: Discrimination and Legal Rights – Rastafari and Religious Protections

Introduction

Though Rastafari is a peaceful, spiritual movement rooted in love, livity, and divine order, Rasta people have historically been the targets of **discrimination, criminalization, and religious suppression** — especially in **state-run systems** like prisons, schools, and workplaces.

From the **cutting of sacred dreadlocks**, to the **denial of Ital meals**, to the refusal to allow head coverings or Nyabinghi gatherings, Rastafari adherents often face **systemic violations of their spiritual rights**. These acts are not just injustices — they are forms of **spiritual violence**.

In this chapter, we'll explore:

PAGE 93

- Common types of discrimination Rasta inmates face;
- Legal frameworks in **Canadian law** that protect Rastafari practice;
- Important legal precedents;
- The spiritual and psychological cost of religious oppression;
- How correctional institutions can turn **discrimination into understanding**.

Common Forms of Discrimination Against Rastafari

Discrimination against Rastas is rarely open or direct — more often, it shows up as **institutional ignorance**, **bureaucratic indifference**, or **cultural bias**.

◆ 1. Denial of Religious Diet (Ital)

Rasta inmates are often told their dietary needs are "preferences" rather than religious necessities. This can lead to:

- Being forced to choose between **eating Babylon food** or **going hungry**;
- Mislabeling Ital as mere veganism;
- Punitive consequences for refusing institutional meals.

◆ 2. Forced Cutting of Dreadlocks

Some prisons enforce grooming policies that conflict with the **Nazirite vow** (see Chapter 3). When dreadlocks are cut or threatened, it is a **spiritual violation** akin to stripping someone of their religious identity.

"You wouldn't tear a yarmulke from a Jew or a turban from a Sikh. Don't cut I locks."

◆ 3. Banning of Head Coverings

Rasta crowns, tams, and wraps are often labeled as contraband or security risks, even though they are sacred. In some cases, inmates are disciplined for refusing to remove them.

◆ 4. No Access to Worship or Religious Materials

Rastas may be:

- Denied time and space for worship;
- Refused access to Rasta literature or the Kebra Nagast;
- Excluded from chaplain services that only recognize mainstream religions.

◆ 5. Mockery, Harassment, or Mislabeling

Rasta inmates are frequently:

- Laughed at or called names like "weedhead" or "Marley";
- Labeled as gang members due to their dreadlocks;
- Seen as "noncompliant" when they follow their religious vows.

The Psychological and Spiritual Cost

Discrimination against Rastas doesn't just affect rights — it affects **souls**. When institutions reject or suppress Rasta livity, the consequences are deep and damaging:

- **Loss of spiritual identity**;
- **Depression, anxiety, or emotional withdrawal**;
- **Loss of trust** in staff or rehabilitative programs;
- **Increased conflict** with administration;
- **Spiritual burnout**, where inmates feel disconnected from Jah.

These outcomes work **against the goals of correctional rehabilitation** and violate **basic human dignity**.

Canadian Legal Protections for Religious Freedom

⚖ The Canadian Charter of Rights and Freedoms

Section 2(a) of the Charter guarantees:

"Freedom of conscience and religion."

This means individuals — including those in prison — have the right to:

- Believe what they choose;
- Express that belief in ritual, dress, diet, and worship;
- Be protected from **government interference** in religious matters.

⚖ Corrections and Conditional Release Act (CCRA)

This law governs federal corrections and explicitly requires institutions to:

- **Respect and accommodate religious practices**;
- Provide **reasonable access** to spiritual advisors and chaplains;
- Ensure that inmates can worship according to their beliefs.

Relevant sections:

- **Section 75**: Religious practice must be accommodated.
- **Section 83**: Chaplaincy services should meet the needs of diverse faith groups.

📖 CSC Commissioner's Directives

Commissioner's Directive 767 requires:

- Recognition of minority religions;
- Protection of sacred items, clothing, and grooming;
- Permission for group worship and religious observances.

Legal Precedents: Rasta Rights in Canadian Courts

While specific Rasta-related prison cases are still under-represented in Canadian case law, the courts have repeatedly upheld the rights of individuals to maintain:

- **Hair and grooming standards** for religious reasons (see *Multani v. Commission scolaire Marguerite-Bourgeoys*, 2006);
- **Religious diets** (see *Singh v. Canada*, 2011, where dietary accommodation was ordered for a Sikh inmate);
- **Religious clothing** (including head coverings) in public institutions.

These cases set a **strong precedent** that **Rastafari religious expression must be respected** under law, and that failure to accommodate may constitute **discrimination under the Canadian Human Rights Act**.

Human Rights Protections

The **Canadian Human Rights Act** prohibits discrimination on the grounds of:

- **Religion or creed**;
- **Race or ethnic origin**;
- **Gender identity and cultural expression**.

This protects Rastas against:

- Systemic mistreatment;
- Cultural erasure;
- Denial of spiritual access.

Rastas who are discriminated against in prison settings **have the right to file human rights complaints** through:

- The Canadian Human Rights Commission;
- The Office of the Correctional Investigator;
- Provincial human rights tribunals.

How Institutions Can Avoid Discrimination

✔ Recognize Rastafari as a Legitimate Religion

This isn't a lifestyle or trend. It's a **faith system** rooted in scripture, culture, and spirituality.

✔ Include Rasta Representation in Policy

Work with Rastafari spiritual advisors or community leaders to ensure that institutional policies reflect **cultural literacy**.

✔ Train Staff to Avoid Bias

Cultural sensitivity training should include **Rastafari practices, vocabulary, and worldview**.

✔ Avoid One-Size-Fits-All Chaplaincy

If chaplains are only trained in Christian theology, they may not recognize or support Rasta needs.

✔ Provide Clear and Accessible Complaint Channels

Inmates should feel safe raising concerns about religious discrimination without fear of retaliation.

Voices from the Faithful

"I no ask for special treatment — just for Babylon to stop violating I livity."

"When I locks were cut, a piece of I soul died that day. They didn't cut hair. They cut I faith."

"Jah give I rights. Babylon can't take what the Most High already bless."

These voices are a **call to conscience** — a reminder that religious liberty is not a privilege, but a **birthright**, even behind bars.

Conclusion

Discrimination against Rastafari in correctional institutions is not just a legal issue — it is a **spiritual crisis**. It denies human dignity, undermines faith, and robs people of the sacred practices that give their lives meaning.

Canadian law provides **strong protections** for religious freedom. It is up to institutions to **honor that law**, not just in policy but in practice — with compassion, cultural literacy, and respect for all faiths.

To truly rehabilitate, institutions must **stop punishing identity** and start **supporting spiritual growth**.

Equal rights and justice — not just in the courts, but in the cells.

*Chapter 14, where we bring it all together with **practical guidance** for correctional staff and administrators. This chapter is about solutions — how to **honor the livity**, protect religious rights, and build **trust and understanding** with Rastafari inmates. This is the **bridge between Babylon and Zion**, built not with bricks but with **respect, training, and cultural competency**.*

📖 Chapter 14: Best Practices for Correctional Staff – Cultural Competency and Respect

Introduction

Working in corrections is a heavy responsibility. Staff are expected to maintain order, enforce policy, and ensure safety. But they're also called to uphold **human rights**, support rehabilitation, and recognize the **diverse spiritual needs** of the people in their care.

When it comes to **Rastafari**, many correctional institutions fall short — not out of malice, but often due to **lack of understanding**. Stereotypes, outdated policies, and unfamiliarity with the faith can lead to violations of rights, unnecessary conflict, and spiritual harm.

This chapter offers **concrete best practices** to help staff:

- Build cultural competence;
- Recognize and respect Rastafari practices;
- Navigate policy and accommodation with fairness;
- Create an environment of **spiritual safety and dignity**.

Because **rehabilitation can't exist without respect.**

Why Cultural Competency Matters

Cultural competency isn't just about learning facts — it's about developing the **skills, attitudes, and awareness** needed to interact respectfully across differences. For Rastafari inmates, staff awareness can be the difference between:

✅ A sacred practice being respected
❌ Or a human rights complaint being filed

✅ Building mutual trust
❌ Or creating ongoing conflict

✅ Supporting rehabilitation
❌ Or enforcing punishment rooted in misunderstanding

1. Understand the Basics of the Faith

All correctional staff — from officers to administrators to chaplains — should receive **basic training** on:

- Rastafari beliefs and worldview;
- Key practices (Nazirite vow, dreadlocks, Ital diet, head coverings);
- Language and communication styles (like "I and I", "overstand", etc.);
- Major holy days and worship formats;
- Importance of nature, music, and livity.

This training helps staff understand that Rasta inmates are not being "difficult" or "noncompliant" — they are practicing a **deeply spiritual path**.

2. Respect Religious Dress and Grooming

Rasta head coverings (crowns, tams, wraps) and dreadlocks are **not fashion statements**. They are sacred symbols, tied to scripture and divine covenant.

Best Practices:

- Allow inmates to wear religious headgear **at all times**, unless there's a **clear security concern**.
- Avoid asking Rasta inmates to **remove headgear in public or group settings** — if removal is absolutely required (e.g., for ID photo), do it **privately**, with dignity, and preferably with **same-gender staff**.
- Never force a Rastafari inmate to cut dreadlocks unless **legally mandated** and no other option exists. Always consult chaplaincy or legal advisors first.

3. Provide Dietary Accommodations

The **Ital diet** is sacred. It's not a preference or fad — it's a religious discipline.

Best Practices:

- Offer **vegan or vegetarian meals free of meat, preservatives, and excessive salt**;
- Clearly label meal options and avoid cross-contamination with non-Ital foods;
- Treat Ital meal requests as **religious accommodations**, not health requests;
- Avoid disciplinary action if an inmate declines meals that violate Ital standards.

If unsure whether a meal meets Ital standards, consult with a chaplain or Rasta advisor.

4. Make Space for Worship and Reasoning

Rastafari worship does not always look like traditional services. It might include:

- Chanting Psalms;
- Reading scripture in small groups;
- Playing Nyabinghi music or spiritual reggae;
- Silent meditation and prayer;
- Reasoning sessions (spiritual group discussions).

Best Practices:

- Provide a space for Rasta inmates to gather regularly for spiritual practice;
- Allow use of audio equipment for **chanting or recorded drumming**;
- Do not restrict worship to only Sunday or Christian chapel formats;
- Invite outside Rasta elders, chaplains, or advisors to guide services when possible.

5. Acknowledge and Accommodate Holy Days

Rasta holy days are sacred. Denying observance can be spiritually harmful.

Best Practices:

- Keep a calendar of Rasta holy days (see Chapter 12);
- Allow time off from work duties or programming for worship;

- Provide special Ital meals or fasting accommodations if requested;
- Encourage chaplains to include Rasta observances in their religious program offerings.

6. Support Access to Spiritual Materials

Faith grows through **knowledge and study**. Incarcerated Rastas need access to:

- The **King James Bible** (preferred translation);
- The **Kebra Nagast** and other Rasta sacred texts;
- Books by and about **Marcus Garvey**, **Haile Selassie**, and **Rasta theology**;
- Audio materials — Nyabinghi chanting, reggae with spiritual messages;
- Writing supplies for **spiritual journaling or poetry**.

Never treat these resources as contraband unless there's a **clear, documented security threat**.

7. Handle Conflict with Sensitivity and Spiritual Awareness

If a Rasta inmate seems "noncompliant," stop and ask:

- Is this **a matter of faith**?
- Are they refusing based on a **sacred vow or spiritual commitment**?
- Have they explained their position clearly?

Avoid using force or punishment when the issue may stem from **religious conviction**. Instead, involve:

- A chaplain;
- A cultural advisor;
- Mediation or reasoning circles.

8. Support Chaplaincy in Serving Rasta Inmates

Chaplains must be prepared to **serve all faiths**, including Rastafari.

Chaplain Best Practices:

- Learn about Rastafari beliefs and practices;
- Consult with Rasta elders or communities outside the institution;
- Support accommodation requests for holy days, diet, grooming, and materials;
- Ensure that worship spaces and times are made available.

9. Promote Institutional Policy That Reflects Inclusion

All policies should reflect:

- **Respect for minority faiths**;
- Clear procedures for **religious accommodation requests**;
- Regular training on **cultural diversity and inclusion**;
- Zero tolerance for **mockery, harassment, or religious profiling**.

10. Listen to the Inmates Themselves

The best teachers are often **those living the faith**.

Create opportunities for Rasta inmates to:

- Educate staff and other inmates;
- Share their faith in group settings;
- Participate in restorative justice circles or cultural programming;
- Write or speak about their experiences.

Lived experience is wisdom.

Voices from Inside

"I'm not resisting. I'm reasoning. I'm not rebelling. I'm practicing I faith."

"The day they let me chant in peace — that was the day I started to heal."

"All I ever wanted was to live how Jah call I to live. That's not too much to ask."

Conclusion

Correctional staff are on the frontlines — not just of justice, but of human dignity. By respecting the faith of Rastafari inmates, they don't just uphold the law — they uphold **love, understanding, and the possibility of transformation**.

Cultural competency isn't weakness — it's **strength in knowledge**. Respect isn't surrender — it's **spiritual leadership**. And when institutions begin to honor **Rasta**

livity, they create space not just for order, but for **redemption**.

Forward with wisdom. Forward with overstanding. **Forward with Rasta.**

---

*We've journeyed through the livity, the law, the worship, and the wisdom — now we step into **the vision**. Chapter 15 is about **restoration, empowerment**, and building a future where **spiritual rehabilitation** isn't just an idea — it's a living reality for Rastafari inmates.*

Let's go. **Final chapter. Final fire.**

📖 Chapter 15: Building Bridges – Supporting Spiritual Rehabilitation for Rastafari Inmates

Introduction

The purpose of corrections should be **restoration** — not just punishment. But too often, the spiritual potential of incarcerated individuals is ignored, disrespected, or blocked. For Rastafari inmates, whose faith is **deeply transformative**, rehabilitation must include **spiritual recognition and cultural inclusion**.

This chapter is about **bridging gaps**: between institutions and inmates, between Babylon and Zion, between judgment and healing. By creating space for Rastafari to thrive in prison, correctional systems can **unlock one of the most powerful forces of change** — a faith that teaches self-control, moral discipline, divine connection, and love for all life.

Let's walk this forward in unity.

Why Spiritual Rehabilitation Matters

Rehabilitation is not just behavioral — it is spiritual.

When someone has lost their way, the path back doesn't come from force or fear. It comes from:

- **Identity**: Knowing who they are in the eyes of the Most High;

- **Purpose**: Believing they have something to live for;
- **Structure**: Rooted in faith-based values;
- **Community**: Reconnecting to others with peace and humility;
- **Responsibility**: Taking ownership of their past and choosing a righteous future.

Rastafari provides all of these. It's not just a belief system — it's a **lifestyle of overstanding, livity, and redemption**.

The Transformative Power of Rastafari

Rastafari teaches the incarcerated:

- To **control the tongue**, speak words of life;
- To **eat clean**, respecting the temple of the body;
- To **respect all life**, walking away from violence;
- To **read scripture**, reflect on justice and deliverance;
- To **chant**, meditate, and reason instead of rage;
- To **stand in dignity**, even in the face of oppression.

When these values are allowed to flourish in prison, they produce:

- [✓] Lower rates of violence and conflict;
- [✓] Increased self-discipline;
- [✓] Improved mental health;
- [✓] Better relationships with staff and inmates;
- [✓] Genuine spiritual growth.

Challenges That Block Rasta Rehabilitation

Despite this potential, Rasta inmates often face **roadblocks** to their spiritual development, such as:

- Denial of religious diet and worship;
- Forced cutting of dreadlocks;
- No access to Rasta literature, elders, or materials;
- Being labeled "noncompliant" when following spiritual vows;
- Mockery or isolation for their appearance or language.

These barriers are not only unjust — they **sabotage the very rehabilitation systems claim to support**.

Building the Bridge: What Rehabilitation Can Look Like

◆ 1. Faith-Based Programming for Rasta Inmates

Rasta inmates should have access to:

- Spiritual study circles;
- Workshops on livity, scripture, and moral reasoning;
- Creative expression rooted in faith (music, poetry, journaling);
- Meditation and mindfulness sessions aligned with Rastafari principles.

These programs must be **designed with the Rasta worldview** in mind — not just "plugging them in" to generic religious groups that don't reflect their beliefs.

◆ 2. Rastafari Spiritual Advisors and Elders

Bring in trained Rasta spiritual advisors — also called **elders** or **priests**, depending on the house (e.g., Nyabinghi, Bobo, Twelve Tribes) — to work with inmates.

They can:

- Lead worship;
- Offer one-on-one spiritual guidance;
- Help resolve faith-based conflicts;
- Educate staff about Rasta livity.

"The presence of an elder in di yard can calm tension and elevate minds."

◆ 3. Restorative Justice from a Rasta Perspective

Rastafari is rooted in justice — not revenge. Concepts like **reparation, redemption, and reconciliation** are deeply woven into the faith. Restorative programs can align with Rasta teachings by:

- Encouraging **accountability** and truth-speaking;
- Promoting **reasoning circles** for conflict resolution;
- Reconnecting offenders to **community responsibility**;
- Honoring **ancestral wisdom** and spiritual values.

◆ 4. Music, Art, and Culture as Spiritual Expression

Allow Rasta inmates to express their faith through:

- Reggae and Nyabinghi chanting;
- Poetry and spoken word;
- Visual arts inspired by Rasta themes;
- Cultural storytelling and history.

These expressions are not hobbies — they are **rituals of healing**, gateways to self-discovery, and affirmations of identity.

◆ 5. Post-Release Support for Rasta Reentry

Faith doesn't end at the gate. Support Rasta inmates as they transition out by:

- Connecting them with **Rasta communities and organizations**;
- Offering continued access to **spiritual mentorship**;
- Providing reentry programs that **respect their livity**;
- Avoiding discrimination based on appearance (locks, dress, speech);
- Partnering with **cultural centers, Ital businesses, and holistic groups.**

Role of Correctional Staff in Supporting Spiritual Growth

Every staff member has a role to play. Support starts with:

- **Listening without judgment;**
- **Asking questions with humility;**
- **Protecting rights with integrity;**
- **Correcting disrespect among colleagues;**
- **Celebrating progress, not just punishing mistakes.**

Staff don't have to **convert or agree** with the faith — only to **respect and protect** its sacredness.

"You don't have to walk the path. Just stop blocking it."

Voices of Rebirth

"I found Rastafari behind bars. I found Jah. I found myself. They locked my body, but they freed my soul."

"They said I was a rebel. But Rasta taught I to be a king."

"Now I speak truth, live Ital, reason with heart. That's the freedom Babylon could never give me."

These stories are the **fruit of spiritual rehabilitation** — lives reclaimed by Jah, through fire and faith.

Conclusion

To truly rehabilitate is to **recognize the spirit behind the man** — not just the sentence, not just the charges, but the soul. Rastafari offers a map out of Babylon's cycle of punishment and into **Zion's promise of transformation**.

Correctional institutions have a choice:

✖ Continue blocking the light of a powerful spiritual path;

☑ Or become partners in redemption, creating space for Rastafari inmates to rise, rebuild, and rejoin society with faith, dignity, and purpose.

The bridge has been built. Now walk it.

Final Words

This book is not just a manual — it's a **call to action**. To walk with respect. To listen with overstanding. To allow faith to do what bars never could: **heal, uplift, and transform.**

More than policy. More than procedure. This is about **people. Purpose. And the power of Jah.**

Forward, Rasta. Always.

Epilogue
"No chains can bind the spirit of the Most High."

This book was not written to explain Rastafari to Babylon. It was written to remind the world that Rastafari lives—in the hearts of the faithful, in the sacred discipline of livity, and even behind the prison gates where the cry for justice still echoes.

Throughout these pages, we have explored the depths of a faith that is often misrepresented or misunderstood. But for the sons and daughters of Zion, Rastafari is not something that needs defending—it simply needs room to grow, to reason, to breathe.

To those working within Correctional Service Canada, the Parole Board, and other institutions of state: You now hold knowledge. Let it become wisdom. True rehabilitation begins with dignity, and dignity begins with respect for the spiritual foundation of all people. Rastafari is not a disruption to order—it is an order unto itself, rooted in peace, love, and divine discipline.

Acknowledgement

I give thanks to the Most High Jah Rastafari for the vision, strength, and guidance that made this work possible.

To the many dedicated individuals working within Correctional Service Canada (CSC) and the Parole Board of Canada — your efforts in creating safer, more humane, and more spiritually inclusive environments do not go unnoticed. Your willingness to engage with faith-based understanding, even when it challenges institutional norms, is a step toward true rehabilitation and justice.

To the chaplains, caseworkers, program officers, and parole agents who walk with open minds and compassionate hearts: this book was written to support you as much as the incarcerated brethren and sistren you serve.

www.ingramcontent.com/pod-product-compliance
Lightning Source LLC
Chambersburg PA
CBHW052053220426
43663CB00012B/2548